Table of Contents

Beyond the Mirror

You Will Be as Successful as YOU Decide to Be

Billy J Riggs

ISBN: 9798230268949
Printed in the United States of America

Preface

The importance of one's self-image has been recognized since the 1950's. There is no shortage of books, workshops, CD's, podcasts, and blog articles promoting self-help theories and gimmicks to improve one's self-image. Unfortunately, many of these articles are about positive thinking and avoiding negativity in life. That advice sounds great, sells books and CD's, and can make you feel better for a while. But personal growth and a durable self-image takes sustained effort until the behavior becomes habitual and subconscious.

This book is intended to serve as a guide that helps the reader map out a pathway to a more positive self-image. It goes beyond personal grooming and learning to dress better in order to improve one's self-perception through compliments from others. Those concepts are important, and indeed are part of the process as detailed in this book. But the methodology discussed in the following chapters has more to do with teleological behavior than instant gratification.

On that note, the fundamental tenets of teleology hold that psychological insights are best gained from the objective observation of outwardly observable human behaviors. What makes teleology unique is its emphasis on the questions of individual free will and self-control. Similar to the study of microeconomics, in which one foregoes immediate profit in favor of long term investments. Similarly, the perspective can be used to identify problematic characteristics that prevent a person from realizing their ideal self.

Another concept discussed and applied throughout this book is that of cybernetics, the scientific study of self-governing and self-regulating systems in human beings. Rest assured that one does not have to be an academic or scientifically gifted to understand, apply, and benefit from cybernetics. In this book, I have attempted to explain how anyone may benefit from a general awareness of cybernetic principles to achieve goals that are important to them.

How You Can Use This Information

Self-image is essential to personality development and human behavior. When you change your self-image, your personality and behavior typically follow in kind. A person's self-image establishes the boundaries of personal accomplishment and defines what you can and cannot do. Development of a realistic self-image will seem to imbue the individual with new talent and capability. This net effect can literally turn failures into success.

Self-image psychology illuminates the power of positive thinking and explains why it seems to work for some but not others. Positive thinking does, in fact, work when it is consistent with an individual's self-image. It literally cannot work when it is inconsistent with an individual's self-image or self-perception. Self-image psychology has proven that the human brain and nervous system function in accordance with cybernetic principles to accomplish established goals of an individual. Your brain and nervous system will work for you as a goal striving mechanism or against you as a failure mechanism depending on how YOU program it.

One of the most significant psychological discoveries of the twentieth century was the self-image. Understanding the nature of the human self-image and one's real self can mean the difference between success and failure, love and hate, bitterness and happiness. Purposeful development of the real self can save a crumbling marriage or reinvigorate a faltering career. On a different level, discovering your real self means the difference between personal freedom and the mindless compulsions of conformity. The choice is yours.

As you read this book, you are asked to participate with the advice given in an effort to help you "experience" the guidance on a personal level. You can gain information by passively reading a book, but intentional experience is active. Purposely interacting with the information in this book, will cause the brain and nervous system to create new neural patterns in the gray matter of the brain.

Rather than providing summary content at the end of each chapter, I would ask you to record the key points you want to remember. Doing your own summaries will help you assimilate the principles and practices discussed in each chapter. For better understanding of the concepts of creating a better self-image, you are also asked to do the suggested exercises consistently for at least 21 days.

Before deciding whether these concepts will work in your life, I ask you to reserve judgment for three to four weeks. You can neither prove nor disprove through intellectual argument the ideas in this book. Therefore, give yourself permission to apply the concepts discussed for at least 21 days before passing judgement. You did not get where you are in life overnight simply by deciding to be where you are. While we cannot accomplish a lifetime of growth in 21 days, you can absolutely experience improvement in that short time. Sometimes the improvement is quite dramatic.

In his bestselling book, *Psycho-Cybernetics*, Maxwell Maltz writes "The self-image is changed, for better or worse, not by intellect alone, but by 'experiencing.' Wittingly or unwittingly, you develop your self-image by your creative experiencing in the past. You can change it by the same method."

Chapter 1

Creating a Successful Self-Image

Your self-image is a mental picture of yourself, both as a physical body and a unique being. When you think about yourself, the feelings and images that come up are important. Whether you consciously recognize it or not, your self-image is an incredibly detailed reflection of the person you believe yourself to be. These reflections have been constructed over the years from our past experiences, failures, successes, childhood interactions, and the way others react to us. Once an idea or perception is added to these experiences, it subconsciously becomes "true" and we behave accordingly.

A common example of success defeating behavior is the student who has learned to believe he or she is not good at math. Subsequently, those beliefs are reflected on a report card or transcript. Or maybe a woman believes herself to be ugly. The reason for the belief does not matter. In social gatherings, she isolates herself from those she perceives to be more attractive, she unconsciously behaves defensively around anyone she perceives might denigrate her. She literally drives people away from herself reinforcing her self-image. Because of this seemingly objective proof, it does not occur to most people that the problem is their own self-image.

Self-image also involves how you feel about your strengths, weaknesses, and abilities. For decades scholars have understood that to really live, that is to find life reasonably satisfying, you must have an adequate and realistic self-image that you can live with. You must find yourself acceptable to you because all your feelings, behavior, and abilities will always be consistent with this self-image. In short, you will live life according to the kind of person you believe yourself to be. That being said, the self-image can be changed. Numerous case histories have demonstrated that one is never too old or too young to change their self-image and go on to live a successful life.

So, what does it mean to be successful? First, it has little to do with common symbols of success such as high end cars, boats, houses and personal bling. Being successful is about personal and professional achievement, fulfillment, and happiness. Historically, successfulness has been defined as "the satisfactory accomplishment of a goal sought after." Human beings are, by nature, purpose driven. Since we are designed to pursue a sense of purpose for our lives, we are often not really content with just existing and maintaining the status quo. We subconsciously know we are meant for something more.

Learning to develop a successful self-image is important because how we think about ourselves affects how we feel about ourselves, and how we interact with others and the world around us. A positive self-image can boost our physical, mental, social, emotional, and spiritual well-being.

It has been taught for decades that nothing succeeds like success. It is true. We learn to be successful by experiencing success. Memories of our past successes are stored and drawn upon to insure successful outcomes of daily tasks. That being said, our brain and nervous system renders the argument "but I have never experienced success," a moot point. Experience can be created.

Experimental and clinical psychologist have long since proven conclusively that the human brain and nervous system cannot tell the difference between an actual experience and one imagined in vivid detail. In later chapters, we will review some controlled clinical experiments where manufactured or synthetic experience was used to improve athletic performance, professional speaking skills, and to establish a competitive edge in business.

The Change Must Be from the Inside Out

One of the reasons it is difficult to change our self-image is because we want to "put on" new ideas like one would put on clothes or a coat. We want to "appear" successful. Too often our efforts to grow or change has to do with wanting a better job, to establish or maintain a relationship, etc.

Many times, when coaching business management personnel, I hear some variation of "I've tried all the positive thinking tricks and they just don' work for me." Almost without exception, the attempt to use positive thinking was applied to some external desire or circumstance such as getting a new job, securing a business loan, starting a business and the like. Very seldom do people think about needing to change their conception of themselves in order to accomplish their goals.

I vividly remember having an ah-ha! moment in college right in the middle of class. I was asked to read the passage in the Bible where Jesus warned listeners about patching an old garment with new material or putting new wine in an old wineskin. As I was reading the text I understood the applicability, that real growth does not come by patching or "putting on" external masks like positive thinking. Positive thinking cannot be applied externally like a patch to improve an inadequate self-image. You simply cannot consistently act or live in a manner that is not consistent with how you see yourself.

Experiments have repeatedly proven that when a person's self-concept is changed, other areas of their lives naturally and easily change to be more consistent with the new self-image. This happens because, psychologically, an individual's ideals and perceptions must appear to be consistent with their self-concept in order to be accepted and true. Ideals and perceptions which are not consistent with the new self-image are subconsciously "not believed" and are not acted on.

Using the student example mentioned earlier, the problem was not that they lacked the required aptitude. They had simply learned to identify with their failures and remembering those perceptions collectively created an inadequate self-image. All too often, instead of saying I failed that test, a factual statement, they wrongly conclude, "I'm a failure." As poor study habits and lack of preparation allow the process to continue, that "failure" perception is reinforced test after test. Performing poorly on a test is something people do; it is not who they are.

A major contributing factor to self-image today is social media. The self-images of many millennials and most generation x, y, and z'ers are dependent on the influence of social media. In many cases, the number of followers a person has determines their self-worth. We are conditioned to project only our best, albeit unrealistic, selves on our social media profiles as a modern way of virtually keeping up with the Joneses.

Not long ago, my millennial daughter deleted her Instagram account. I couldn't understand why a young person would ever do such a thing, so I asked, and her response caught me off-guard. The pressure of taking the right picture, with the right filter, wearing the right outfit, at the right place, with the right people was too much pressure. She was frustrated that no matter what she posted, someone always had something negative to say about it. Her self-image was becoming dependent upon what other people said about her posts.

Regardless of whether you realize it, you're spending a great deal of time and effort on the creation of your digital identity. The molding of this alternate self depends heavily on how others are projecting themselves in these arenas as well. What happens to your 'real' self, then?

Social media puts an interesting lens on the creation of the self, and how this construct affects our mental well-being. The ideal self is the self we aspire to be. My ideal self would be a 50-year-old successful freelance writer who travels the world giving free workshops on self-worth and leadership.

One's self-image is the person we actually are; based on the actions, behaviors, and habits currently possessed. According to Carl Rogers's theory of personality, every human has the basic instinct to improve him or herself and realize their full potential. Abraham Maslow called this achievement self-actualization. He believed this state was attained when the ideal self and the person's self-image were in line with each other. This person would be deemed a fully functioning person.

Each of us carries what Robert Firestone termed the critical inner voice. It is a dynamic that exists within every individual that offers a negative filter through which to view our life. It is theorized that the voice is created at an early age during times of stress or trauma.

Social media is not only extremely pervasive, it is an activity in which you are expected to participate. This phenomenon is a tangible version of Rogers's concept of the ideal self. We have a general persona we construct and put out to the cyber universe based on the person we want to be, and more important, based on the person we want to be seen as.

The Elements of Our Self-Image

Our self-image is influenced by how we believe others see us and how we measure up to our own standards. Our self-esteem, the way we feel about ourselves, is directly affected by our perception of our self. Having a poor self-image, and consequently low self-esteem, can get in the way of our relationships with others.

If you don't like yourself, it can be difficult to like or love someone else, according to therapist and couple's counselor Julia Cole in "Loving Yourself, Loving Another." This is because it can be difficult for someone with low self-esteem to accept that someone would love them. Your self-image can also affect how you communicate with others. Having a positive self-image means you're confident enough to own up to your mistakes. For example, if you get into an argument with your partner, you can recognize where you may have contributed to the misunderstanding and apologize with the comfort that you are not perfect and the confidence that you can improve.

There are certainly times, it seems, that when other people have what you want, they win, and you lose. However, in most cases, there is enough success for everyone. Change your frame of reference from win-lose to win-win and think to yourself that if one person can succeed, so can others, including you. Focusing your thoughts and energies on what needs to be done to achieve your goals will leave you with less time to concern yourself with envy.

People like positive feedback, and they also like the people who give them positive feedback. You can change the negative impact of a negative perception by praising those you may be jealous of. Find something meaningful to compliment them on, relevant to the conversation, and see how that changes your interactions with them. You may even find that they offer you some help toward achieving your own goals.

Self-respect is another element of one's self-image that every person should have, but unfortunately not everyone does. Self-respect is acceptance of yourself as a whole person. It doesn't mean you think you're perfect; in fact, we all deserve respect even though we are not perfect. Self-respect means you hold yourself to your own standards, and you try not to worry too much about what other people think of you.

If you know you lack these qualities, it's never too late to learn to believe in yourself and learn self-respect. When you learn to love yourself and treat others with respect, you'll feel an amazing sense of inner satisfaction. People will also begin to seek you out to spend time with you, as they will see you as a role model for how they would like to behave. The result is increased self-respect and confidence.

Self-confidence is an attitude about your skills and abilities. It means you accept and trust yourself and have a sense of control in your life. You know your strengths and weakness well and have a positive view of yourself. You set realistic expectations and goals, communicate assertively, and can handle criticism.

What is your self-worth? Some people feel the need to flaunt their wealth, education, or good looks in order to receive the validation they need to feel like they're important. These people often feel the need to belittle others in order to feel better about themselves. A person who has dignity and self-respect does not behave like this. A dignified individual, who respects him or herself, knows their own worth without needing to put others down to feel important.

Your sense of self-worth helps you to trust your own judgment and make better decisions, which are important leadership qualities that can help you advance in your career. Self-worth can lend you the confidence to run meetings, support other team members, and have greater autonomy at work.

A person who has dignity does not need to start rumors, manipulate others, and cause drama to be noticed. A dignified person stands out from the crowd because of the positive contributions he makes to the lives of others. He feels fulfilled because he knows he's done nice things for others, and he doesn't need to broadcast his good deeds to other people for validation.

Be aware of how much you complain about your life to others. If every conversation that you have involves criticizing yourself and others, this is a sign that you have low self-respect. Instead, make conversations revolve around positivity such as giving genuine compliments to others, talking about steps you've made to improve parts of your life that you weren't satisfied with and showing appreciation when you receive gifts and praise from others.

A person who respects themselves doesn't allow negative events in their life to bring them down. Instead, it's important to take difficult moments and turn them into productivity. Determine what went wrong and use that as motivation to turn it into something positive. Mistakes and rejections are learning opportunities that can be used to improve yourself in the future. A person with a successful self-image takes these events in stride, knowing that things will get better, because they believe in themself.

Learning to Use Your Subconscious Mind

The science of cybernetics has repeatedly proven that what we call the subconscious mind acts as an automatic goal-striving mechanism, a human "servo-mechanism" that moves us toward a predetermined goal. This servo-mechanism consists of the brain and nervous system and is controlled by the conscious mind. The subconscious mind functions similar to the way an onboard navigation system operates in a guided missile or torpedo.

Actually, the human subconscious mind is not a mind at all. It is a complex, creative, impersonal, goal striving mechanism that we "program" and control via the information we put into it. This creative mechanism will work automatically and impersonally to achieve our goals of happiness and success or unhappiness and failure, depending on the goals set for it by our conscious mind.

Like any other servo-mechanism, our subconscious creative mind must have clear, detailed objectives to reach. These detailed objectives are goals that we set for ourselves and feed into our creative mechanism through our thoughts, beliefs, and interpretations of events and circumstances around us. Through our attitudes and interpretations of life events, we describe the problem to be solved to our subconscious mind.

Practical Application. Take a few minutes to write down the main elements of a successful self-image. How do you see yourself now, and how do you want to be in the near future? How do you want to be perceived by others? Your self-image goals must be detailed and unambiguous. We will address how to train your automatic success mechanism to reach these goals in the following chapters.

Chapter 2
Freeing Yourself from False Beliefs

> **"Whatever we plant in our subconscious mind and nourish with repetition and emotion will one day become a reality."** — *Earl Nightingale*

What are false beliefs? They are beliefs we have about ourselves that are untrue and limiting. They live in our subconscious and since 90 percent of our actions stem from our subconscious, our false beliefs play a huge role in nearly everything we do. Also, since they live in our subconscious, we may not be fully aware of how they affect our daily lives.

For example, if you believe you are unlovable, you may sabotage relationships, hold on when you shouldn't, or avoid getting into relationships. Logical reasoning may provide you with explanations on why you are doing this, when at the core, it's fueled by your false belief that you are unlovable. Our behavior stems from our beliefs. And good or bad, what your life looks like is a result of your collective behavior over time.

If we change or dissolve our false beliefs, we can change our behavior and ultimately change our life. Once you have identified your false belief engrams, you can start to rewire them and transform them into successful self-perceptions. There are many different ways and theories on how to rewire yourself. Let's start with an explanation of what an engram is.

An engram is a segment of cognitive information inside the brain, theorized to be the means by which memories are stored as biophysical or biochemical changes in the brain and other neural tissue in response to external stimuli. The actions you take on a daily basis are heavily influenced by the patterns absorbed by your subconscious mind. What you say, what you do, and how you feel are all guided by your subconscious beliefs and interpretations.

If you have ever found yourself doing or saying something that is not aligned with your conscious beliefs or desires, it is most likely because the engrams in your subconscious mind have been previously programmed differently by you and the people/things around you.

Our subconscious mind is the underlying auto-pilot feature in our brain. It soaks up information just like a sponge. Beginning from the time that we are born until about 7 or 8 years old, your subconscious formed a foundation of your preset beliefs and perceptions based on the people around you, the music you listened to, and the TV shows and movies you watched.

The thing is, your subconscious mind didn't just stop taking in information because you've aged, in fact, you only really ever become aware of these patterns when they begin to hinder your progress and productivity in your everyday life. Now that you're an adult, you may have noticed some habits, thought patterns, and natural instincts that no longer positively serve you. You may even end up sabotaging yourself because of them.

The Power of a False Belief

The following story was told by Maxwell Maltz in his book titled, *Adventures in Staying Young*. Dr. Maltz gave a detailed case history of how "Mr. Russell" aged 20 years almost overnight because of a false belief, then regained his youth almost as quickly when he accepted the truth. While it is a long story, I have included it here because it exemplifies the power of the human belief system.

> "I performed a cosmetic operation on Mr. Russell's lower lip for a very modest fee, under the condition that he must tell his girlfriend that the operation had cost him his entire savings of a lifetime. His girlfriend had no objection to him spending money on her, insisted that she loved him, but explained she could never marry him because of his too-large lower lip. However, when he told her this and proudly exhibited his new lower lip, her reaction was just as I had expected, but not as Mr. Russell had anticipated."

"She became hysterically angry, called him a fool for having spent all his money, and advised him in no uncertain terms that she had never loved him and never would, and that she had merely played him for a sucker as long as he had money to spend on her. However, she went further than expected. In her anger and disgust she also announced that she was placing a Voodoo curse upon him."

"Both Mr. Russell and his girlfriend had been born on an island in the West Indies where Voodoo was practiced by the ignorant and superstitious. His family had been rather well-to-do. His background was one of culture and he was a college graduate. Yet, when in the heat of anger, his girlfriend "cursed" him, he felt vaguely uncomfortable but did not think too much about it."

However, he remembered and wondered when a short-time later he felt a strange small hard bump on the inside of his lip. A friend who knew of the Voodoo curse insisted that he see a "Dr. Smith," who promptly assured him that the bump inside his lip was the feared "African Bug," which would slowly eat away all his vitality and strength."

"Mr. Russell began to worry and looked for signs of waning strength. He was not long in finding them. He lost his appetite and his ability to sleep. I learned all this from Mr. Russell when he returned to my office several weeks after I had dismissed him. My nurse didn't recognize him, and no wonder."

"The Mr. Russell who had first called upon me had been a very impressive individual. He stood about six foot four, a large man with the physique of an athlete, and the bearing and manner that bespoke an inner dignity and gave him a magnetic personality. The very pores of his skin seemed to exude an animal-like vitality."

"The Mr. Russell who now sat across the desk from me had aged at least 20 years. His hands shook with the tremor of age. His eyes and cheeks were sunken. He had lost about 30 pounds. The changes in his appearance were all characteristic of the process which medical science, for want of a better name, calls 'aging.'"

After a quick examination of his mouth I assured Mr. Russell I could get rid of the African Bug in less than 30 minutes, which I did. The bump which had caused all the trouble was merely a small bit of scar tissue from his operation. I removed it, held it in my hand, and showed it to him. The important thing is that he saw the truth and believed it. He gave a sigh of relief, and it seemed as if there was almost an immediate change in his posture and expression. Several weeks later, I received a nice letter from Mr. Russell, together with a photo of him and his new bride. He had gone back to his home and married his childhood sweetheart. The man in the picture was the first Mr. Russell. He had grown young again – overnight."

"A false belief had aged him 20 years. The truth had not only set him free of fear and restored his confidence but had actually reversed the aging process. If you could have seen Mr. Russell as I did, both before and after, you would never again entertain any doubt the power of belief, or that an idea accepted as truth from any source, can be immensely powerful."

It is not the end of the world if these scenarios sound familiar. It just means that you will have to take the time to reprogram your negative subconscious beliefs, thoughts, and habits. Take the time to ask yourself, what are you downloading into your mind? Do you have a positive or negative self-image based on your external environment growing up? Do you often get frustrated and overwhelmed by your own negative thought patterns? Reprogramming your mind for success will help solve many of these issues and shift your mind to a more focused and limitless belief system.

Your Brain is Designed to Reinforce Your Beliefs and Regulate Your Life

Your subconscious mind uses something called a homeostatic impulse, which regulates functions like body temperature, heartbeat and breathing. Brian Tracy explained it like this: "Through your autonomic nervous system, your homeostatic impulse maintains a balance among the hundreds of chemicals in your billions of cells so that your entire physical machine functions in complete harmony most of the time."

But what many people don't realize is that just as your brain is built to regulate your physical self, it also regulates your mental self. Your mind is constantly filtering and bringing to your attention information and stimuli that affirms your preexisting beliefs as well as presenting you with repeated thoughts and impulses that mimic and mirror that which you've done in the past. Psychologists refer to this filtering and reinforcing as confirmation bias.

Your subconscious mind is also the realm in which you can either habituate yourself to expect, and routinely seek the actions that would build and reinforce, success, happiness, and wholeness, or failure and unhappiness. The first step in creating massive change in your life is not actually believing that it's possible, it's being willing to see if it is possible.

Give Yourself Permission to be Successful.

Instead of regurgitating the same old narrative of believing you'll be happy once you will the lottery, get a promotion, or some other vague "if then," work on changing your inner monologue to: "It's okay for me to be successful and live a good life."

Give yourself permission to be happy and successful and not feel guilty about it. If you have a subconscious association between success and being amoral, or corrupt, of course you're not going to do what you need to do to live the life you want to live. Instead, give yourself permission to step into a whole, happy, healthy, grounded, and meaningful existence.

You are not going to be able to jump from being a complete skeptic to a wholehearted believer. The step between those belief systems is being open to seeing what could be possible. The point being that you're willing to see if change is possible, that's what will change your life.

Create a Master Plan for Your Life.

I'm not talking about writing out a five or ten year plan for your life. Too many things change too quickly these days. It is nearly impossible to set realistic goals that you'll be able to keep. Most likely, new or even better opportunities will surface, and though your life won't look like you thought it would, you will likely be better off for that.

Instead, have a master plan. Identify your core values and motivations. Ask yourself; What is the ultimate goal? What do you want to accomplish while you are alive? What kind of legacy do you want to leave? Once you have your non-negotiable values identified, you can make decisions for the long-term that align with your true self.

Being able to imagine what it is you want out of your life is absolutely essential for creating it, because if you don't know where you're going, you won't know which way to turn first or when you get there. Once you have a crystal clear image in your mind of what you want and how you want to live, you are then capable of beginning to enact and create it. If you are still unclear or uncertain about what you want, you will likely be incapable of taking real, meaningful action toward anything.

You cannot develop a new self-image by simply deciding to, or by will power alone. Your subconscious mind needs a reason or justification that your current self-image is in error and that a new self-image is needed. You cannot simply imagine a new self-image unless you sincerely feel that it is based on truth. Science has confirmed what philosophers and other intuitive people have long declared: Every human being is literally engineered for success by his creator.

Every human being has access to a power greater than himself. Some refer to this power as God. Some simply consider it the universe. Some call it the Ether, a sort of universal energy. If you were engineered for success and happiness, then any perception of yourself as unworthy of happiness, or of a person who was meant to struggle, must be in error.

Practical Application: Read this chapter through at least twice a week for the next three weeks. Look for examples in your past experiences of how false beliefs have been subconsciously created and may still be influencing your decisions and experiences. The truth of the concepts in this chapter can set you free from an old and inadequate self-image, if you read it often and take it to heart.

Next, write down 3-5 false beliefs that came to mind as you read this chapter. Then write down the truth regarding yourself and those old beliefs. For example: "I NEED strong coffee in order to function in the morning." Correction – I USE strong coffee to get started in the morning, but I do not NEED it. Drinking ice water will have the same effect. I drink coffee because I like it.

Chapter 3

You Are Wired for Success

In the same way you do not need to be an electrical engineer to operate a light switch, you do not need a degree in physics, neuroscience, or any other field to operate your own servomechanism. You DO however need to be familiar with the following principles transliterated from Dr. Maltz's work in cybernetics. Commit them to memory and they will bring understanding to what follows in this book.

Principle 1. Your built-in success mechanism must have a clearly defined goal or target that already exists. Your servomechanism will steer you to a target that already exists or steer you to discover a goal that already exists. Your automatic success mechanism is teleological in nature, meaning it must be oriented toward an end result, a clearly defined goal.

Principle 2. Do not be concerned about making mistakes or having temporary setbacks. Servomechanisms operate by moving forward until it receives negative feedback then making corrections and continuing on toward its goal. Also, try not to get distracted with figuring out how your servo-mechanism will accomplish the goals you set for it. Stay focused on the end goal, the desired result, and the "how" will be provided or made clear at the appropriate time.

Principle 3. Learn to trust your subconscious mind (your servomechanism). Learning a new skill is largely accomplished by trial and error, making corrections, and trying again until the desired outcome is achieved. With repetition, your subconscious servomechanism will learn new success habits and forget, or overwrite, previous negative outcomes. To put it another way, you must learn to let your creative mechanism do what you have programmed it to do without concern for whether it is working or not or trying to force an outcome through your conscious effort.

Letting your creative mechanism work spontaneously, according to present need, instead of trying to "make" it work, will be more challenging for some personalities than others. However, this trust is necessary because your creative mechanism works below the level of consciousness. You simply cannot know what is going on in your subconscious. The creative mechanism operates as you act and as demands are placed on it by circumstances in your life. Don't wait for conclusive proof. Behave as if it is there and it will be. As Emerson said, "Do the thing and you will have the power."

Use Your Imagination

As mentioned previously, your brain and nervous system cannot tell the difference between a real experience and a vividly imagined experience. In both instances it will respond automatically to information you give it from your forebrain. The brain and nervous system react appropriately to what you think or imagine to be true. Therefore, your imagination plays a far more significant role than you might realize.

Creative imagination is not something reserved for poets, artists, or inventors. We use our imagination almost constantly. Most importantly, we use our creative imagination to set goals and create the image our automatic mechanism continuously strives to achieve. Contrary to popular belief, we act, or fail to act, not based on our will, but based on what we "imagine" to be true about ourselves and our environment. It is the way we are designed to operate. To illustrate this concept, consider how hypnosis influences a person's imagination, which in turn influences their behavior.

To the lay person, there seems to be something paranormal at work in their minds. In fact, what we see is the normal operating process of the human brain and nervous system. When a compliant hypnotic subject is repeatedly told the temperature outside is dropping quickly as a cold front approaches, not only will they appear to be cold or begin to shiver, but their skin will also get goose bumps in response to their belief that it is cold.

University and clinical studies have found that hypnotized subjects are able to do surprising things only when convinced that the hypnotist's words are true statements. Once the subject is convinced the hypnotist's words are true statements, they behave differently because they believe differently. It turns out that it is a good thing that we feel and act according to what we believe or imagine to be true.

The human brain and nervous system are designed to react automatically to problems and challenges in the environment. For example, if you were walking along a wooded trail and came across a grizzly bear, you do not need to "decide" to be afraid. The fear response is automatic and appropriate. First your brain automatically goes in to fight or flight mode, dumping large amounts of adrenaline into your blood stream enabling you to run faster than you've ever ran before. Your heartbeat is quickened in preparation for the extra load on the cardiovascular system. All bodily functions not relevant to running and life support are shut down.

While many of us learned about these biological responses in high school, what most people do not realize is that the brain and nervous system that reacts to our immediate or imagined environment is the same brain and nervous system that tells us what the environment "is." In the aforementioned example, what was subconsciously believed or imagined to be true about the environment that caused the automatic response.

We act and feel according to the "images" in our mind of what things are, rather than what they really are. We have certain images of our self, our world, and the people around us, and we behave as though the images we hold are reality, rather than the things the images represent. So, logically, if our ideas, beliefs, and mental images of ourselves are distorted or unrealistic, then our responses to our environment will likewise be inappropriate.

Imagine Yourself Successful

Take a moment to think about where you are and where you want to be, then imagine the action steps that you will have to take to get there. Implement these action steps in your life by creating a maintainable daily routine in order to make that change happen. Top performers in any profession, business, or sport, regardless of socioeconomic status, know the importance of imagining or visualizing themselves succeeding in their minds before they ever do in reality.

When you think of a big goal or dream that you want to achieve, it's natural to think of all of the obstacles that will come your way. The problem is that we often allow these obstacles to become so big in our minds that it inhibits us from moving forward. This is when many become satisfied with mediocrity.

The key is to make your positive vision stronger than anything that can set you back. The more vividly imagined, the better it will work for you. Start thinking of your personal goals in life in precise detail. Picture what you will do once your goal is reached. How does it feel? How will this change the course of your life? Remember, your brain and nervous system cannot tell the difference in a real and an imagined experience. The little details increase the likelihood of achieving the big picture.

Realizing that our actions, feelings, and behavior are the result of our own mental images and beliefs gives us the conditions we need for changing personality, gaining skills, and attaining success and happiness. Many of the habits and thought patterns we currently possess aren't even our own, they actually belong to the environments that we were either raised in or have put ourselves in. However, this doesn't eliminate our responsibility of breaking those cycles for our own overall well-being.

Release your attachment to the "how." Your job is to identify the what, and then allow your subconscious to work in tandem with your environment for the how. For example: If your goal is to work remotely and run your own business, instead of giving up if your first attempt fails, try reimagining how else you could achieve your ultimate vision in a new way that is more financially lucrative. The point is that life will always surprise you with how things come to fruition. Instead of being obsessively attached to every little detail working out the way you think it should, trust your success mechanism to steer you toward your clearly defined goal, your mental picture.

Does Imagining Success Really Work?

People have been using their imaginations to improve their gaming skills, sales meetings, golf scores, and more for decades. It was once believed that chess champion, Capablanca, was unbeatable in match play. Then, a relatively unknown player, Alekhine, challenged Capablanca and defeated him. It was later discovered that Alekhine had prepared himself for the match much like a boxer prepares himself for a major fight. Alekhine isolated himself for three months, ate healthily, stopped drinking and smoking, followed a calisthenics routine, and played chess with Capablanca, in his mind, every day.

Successful salespeople use imagination and visualization to increase their sales percentages through role playing. Selling is generally a matter of situational awareness. Successful salespeople use their down time to imagine themselves in various situations with potential customers and practice listening techniques, overcoming every sort of objection, and satisfying customer concerns before they ever sit down with them in person.

Most people get at least a little anxious before a job interview. Whether you are interviewing for a new job or being considered for a promotion at your current company, the uncertainty of an interview can be unnerving. Psychologists, career coaches, and human resource professional recommend rehearsal practice as way to plan for the interview.

Go over the various questions you think the interviewer might ask in your mind and respond to each question as if you were sitting in front of them. Do your research on the company or the position you are interviewing for. Rehearse the entire interview in your mind from your arrival at the meeting through its conclusion. Even if none of the questions you anticipated come up, the rehearsal practice will still be beneficial to you. You will be more confident and relaxed during the interview.

Even though real life does not follow a pre-written script like a stage play, practicing the interview in your imagination will help you ad lib and respond more spontaneously because you will have practiced spontaneous responses to seemingly random questions. You don't have to be an actor, but we are always "acting" in one role or another throughout our lives. Why not rehearse and act the role of a successful person?

Since the beginning of time, successful men and women have used mental pictures and imaginative rehearsal practice to achieve success. In their book, *Making the Most of Your Life*, Ewing Webb and John Morgan explain that Napoleon spent his years on the island of Corsica imagining himself as a commander and even drew maps of the island that included defensive armament placements with mathematically precise placement.

As a boy Conrad Hilton "played hotel" imagining himself as a hotel operator long before he bought his first hotel. Similarly, entrepreneur and ship builder, Henry J. Kaiser often said that each of his business ideas were fully developed in his imagination before they became a reality. In addition to being known as the father of modern ship building, some of those ideas became Kaiser Aluminum, Kaiser Steel Company, and Kaiser Automotive (the American origin of the compact car).

You Can Live Your Dreams

The science of Cybernetics gives us an insight into why mental picturing produces amazing accomplishments and how these successes are the result of the natural and normal functioning of our subconscious mind and brain.

Cybernetics regards the human brain, nervous system, and muscular system collectively as an extraordinarily complex automatic goal-seeking mechanism which steers us toward a desired target or goal using feedback from our environment and stored information to automatically correct course as necessary. To be clear, I do not mean to imply that human beings are machines, rather than your physical brain and nervous system functions like a machine or computer that is programmed and operated by you.

It is important to remember that this automatic creative mechanism only works when it has a clearly defined target or goal to work toward. You must first clearly see a thing in your mind before you can do it. When you see a goal clearly in your mind, the creative success mechanism of your mind takes over much better and more efficiently than you can do it by conscious effort or willpower.

It is also important to remember that focusing on the clearly defined mental picture and "letting" your creative mechanism work does not relieve you of putting in the effort and work. While your imagination can lay out the path to your target, you must put in the effort to pay attention to environmental queues and follow the insight of your subconscious mind.

In her book titled, *Prescription for Anxiety*, Dr. Leslie Weatherhead stated, "If we have in our minds a picture of ourselves as fear-haunted and defeated nobodies, we must get rid of that picture at once and hold up our heads. That is a false picture and the false must go. God sees us as men and women whom, and through whom, He can do a great work. He sees us as already serene, confident, and cheerful. He sees us not as pathetic victims of life, but as masters of the art of living; not wanting sympathy, but imparting help to others, therefore thinking less of ourselves, and full, not of self-concern, but of love and laughter and a desire to serve...Let us look at the real selves which are in the making the moment we believe in their existence. We must recognize the possibility of change and believe in the self we are in the process of becoming. That old sense of unworthiness and failure must go. It is false, and we are not to believe in what is false."

Practical Application: Your present self-image was built in your own imagination by your evaluations and interpretations of your life experiences thus far. Now you are to build a more successful self-image through the same process. Set aside 30 minutes each day to be alone and undisturbed. Make yourself comfortable, close your eyes, and exercise your imagination.

Perhaps imagine yourself in an empty movie theatre and your life is playing on the big screen. It is important that your pictures approximate reality as much as possible. Notice and take care to include the small details, sounds, smells, how you are dressed, how you act and interact appropriately with objects and other people. The more you rehearse the self-image and life you want, the more natural it will become as you create the "memories" and engrams of that self-image.

Write down the key points of interest to you from this chapter and your own example of how they have applied in your past.

Chapter 4

Change Core Beliefs with Rational Thinking

There is a commonly accepted fallacy, lingering from the 19th and early 20th century practice of psychoanalysis, that logical, rational, conscious thinking is somehow separate from unconscious automatic processes. It implies that negative beliefs, feelings, and behaviors cannot be changed without months of allegedly therapeutic dredging of the subconscious to uncover the basis of personal beliefs, feelings, and behaviors.

However, modern science has proven conclusively that the automatic success mechanism, or subconscious mind, is absolutely impersonal. It has no separate will of its own. It only responds to your current beliefs about yourself and your environment. It appropriately, and only, works on the ideas, beliefs, interpretations, and opinions you feed into it. It will always seek to accomplish the goals that you consciously focus on through conscious thought.

The first step in changing a false core belief is to actually identify why the belief is false. What you will find when you look at an issue is that mental agreements usually come in bundles. When you do a thorough job of identifying your core beliefs you are more than halfway to changing them. This task can be a little challenging in the beginning but gets easier with practice.

Identifying a core belief is like solving a mystery of the illusions in your mind. You have to follow some clues to get down to the hidden beliefs in the unconscious. Let's use the example of fear of public speaking. Fear of public speaking isn't a core belief. It is an emotional reaction to a belief. The thought a person has is, "They will think I'm an idiot." This is the fear, but not the belief. Fears associated with what other people think of us are quite common.

This same dynamic can occur in the mind when asking for a raise, asking someone out on a date, or meeting new people. However, the thought is not a core belief. One has to be careful here because they are often misleading. When solving a crime, you follow the money. When finding core beliefs, you follow the emotion. We have to keep questioning how the emotion of fear is created by the act of what someone else thinks.

If someone pointed at your hair, claimed it was green, and then started to laugh at how silly you looked, would you feel hurt? Probably not. When you know your hair is not naturally green you would know this person is just being silly, on drugs, or having problems with their vision. You know the issue is with their perception, and not with you.

If you don't genuinely believe you look foolish, you are less affected by what others think. Understanding that others' perception of you, is not you, gives you freedom from their opinion. It only matters if we believe and accept other people's perceptions as truth. It is the fear of emotional pain that results from believing something negative about our self. What other people think is just a trigger that activates our own negative core beliefs.

The reality is that we don't know what people are thinking. We usually assume what they think about us and then believe our assumption. The point is, to identify our core beliefs we have to look beyond the thoughts we think. These hidden assumptions are not apparent from the reaction or the thoughts. We have to get past the surface of thoughts, and our reaction to them, to find our beliefs.

Changing Core Beliefs

Our mind is quick to make this association and believe the opinions other people have about us. We often believe it without realizing it. However, this influence starts to fall apart under some scrutiny. First, understand that you couldn't possibly be what other people conceptualize in their mind and that you don't have the power to accurately read another person's mind either.

When you identify the core beliefs to this detail they begin to become ridiculous. When you fully identify a set of false, or no longer true, beliefs you instinctively divest your belief in them. This is an automatic response of your subconscious due to your expanded awareness. Just by identifying your beliefs, you facilitate change in your emotions and behavior without a lot of work.

Different people will have different opinions about you. Their opinions are mental concepts in *their* mind. You, your self-image, is not equivalent to the mental concept in another person's mind. Some people might change their mental opinion about you after spending some time with you, and yet you didn't change. We only feel a change when we change our belief about ourselves. Someone else's opinion is only a trigger to activate our different core beliefs.

I realize the concepts described in this chapter seem simple enough but changing core beliefs does require some work. There is also one especially important step in the process that is often missed. You have to change your point of view in order to change a core belief. Where you shift your point of view in your mind is critically important. Certain points of view will make it easy to dissolve a core belief and others will stop the process.

A Paradigm Shift

A faster and easier way to change a belief is through shifting your point of view, a paradigm shift. A new perspective allows you to have that epiphany of awareness that changes the way you see things. When you are within the paradigm of a false belief, it appears completely true, so you continue to believe in it. This is one of the problems with simply using affirmations to adjust your self-image. From the point of view of our existing beliefs, our affirmations look like a lie. We can end up feeling like a liar or a fraud trying to adopt new beliefs that go against our current paradigm.

A belief paradigm acts very much like a dream when you are asleep. When you are in a vivid dream it can seem completely real. Your servomechanism reacts as if what is happening in the dream is really happening to you. You might feel like your life is in danger and feel the corresponding emotions of fear. But then you wake up from the dream. You begin looking at the dream from the perspective of sitting up in your bed in an awakened state. With that shift in point of view, you immediately drop your fear and the notion that you are in danger. With this shift in perspective, the illusion of the dream no longer has power over your mind and emotions. Changing your point of view in this way allows you to quickly change beliefs.

Every adult human being has memories of past failures, unpleasant memories, or painful experiences. It is not necessary to dig up and examine past events in order to effect personality changes. As stated in the previous chapter, all skill learning is accomplished through trial and error. That is, trying, missing the mark, noting the degree of error, making necessary corrections, making another attempt, and repeating the process until success is achieved. Then, the successful pattern is remembered and employed on future efforts.

This process is natural and true for anyone learning to play horseshoes, throw darts, sing in tune, drive a car, play golf, get along with other people, and every other skill. It is also true of machine learning. All servomechanisms retain "memories" of past errors, failures, and negative experiences. These negative experiences do not inhibit, rather they contribute to, the learning process, as long as they are used appropriately as minor deviations from the desired goal.

As soon as an error is recognized, and course corrections made, the error should be consciously forgotten, and the successful achievement remembered. Our past mistakes and failures were a natural and necessary part of the learning process that helped our automatic success mechanism steer us toward positive outcomes. When they have served their purpose, they should be forgotten. If we consciously dwell on our mistakes or continue to feel guilty of making the mistake, the mistake or failure itself becomes the goal in our imagination and memory and that will become the focus of our servomechanism.

You Have the Power to Change Your Beliefs

Has it ever occurred to you that you can change your foundational beliefs? Most people subconsciously believe something along the lines of, "With my background and lack of education, I am already doing about as well as anyone ever expected." The majority of people on the planet barely get by as they go through the motions of life. While most people occasionally wonder if there's more to life than what they're experiencing, they don't believe they can change their lives to any significant degree. That's the power of belief.

Our beliefs, whether we create them ourselves or we get them from our family and friends, form the basis of our understanding of the world around us. Many people stick with their beliefs all their life. Consequently, their lives, which are the manifestation of their beliefs, don't change much over the years. Here's what a few notable thinkers of our time believe:

Mahatma Gandhi, the leader of India's nonviolent independence movement, *"If I have the belief that I can do it, I shall surely acquire the capacity to do it even if I may not have it in the beginning."*

Philosopher William James said, *"Believe that life is worth living and your belief will help create the fact."*

And Mark Victor Hansen, author of Chicken Soup for the Soul, *"Your belief determines your action and your action determines your results, but first you have to believe."*

But this isn't about what philosophers, authors or world leaders say or have experienced. It's about YOU, your beliefs, and changing the ones that limit you. You are the expert who, for every moment of every day of your life, has been collecting the data on how your beliefs affect your life. Your belief system is based on your evaluation of something.

Generally speaking, if we reevaluate a situation, our belief about the situation will change. So, start to evaluate your beliefs from different perspectives. If you do that, you may find that many of your beliefs are baseless. First, think of something you struggle with. Ask yourself why the situation is difficult for you. Then, think about what you believe about the situation. Next, ask yourself how someone you admire would perceive the situation. What would that person's beliefs be? How would your experiences or results would be different if you adopted their beliefs? Then, start to approach things from the new perspective whenever the situation comes up to see how it affects your results.

Think about a recurring situation that upsets you. Write down the belief that causes you to react negatively. Take a few minutes to think about or write down the reasons the belief is false. Keep those reasons in mind each time the situation occurs until you are no longer bothered by it. Once you get started in evaluating your beliefs, you will realize that you can achieve anything you want. Whether you choose to pursue what you want is entirely up to you. Should you choose to devote yourself to the ongoing journey of evaluating your beliefs, you will likely develop a higher level of joy and respect for who you really are and what you're capable of.

Practical Application: The following exercise is intended to help you evaluate some of your beliefs and for seeing your beliefs from different angles. Try to not take yourself too seriously and honestly look at your beliefs with an open and expanded mind.

1. Consider a situation or belief that troubles or limits you.
2. Evaluate the belief, write down your thoughts (e.g., ask where it came from, if it's really true, if it's helping you grow, etc.) and determine what a more empowering belief would be in that situation.
3. Create a detailed statement of the belief or perspective you want and re-evaluate the situation with this new belief.

4. Practice entering the situation with the new belief over and over again, until you embody the new perspective.

Chapter 5

Why You Can Trust Your Subconscious Mind

"The faculty of imagination is the great spring of human activity, and the principal source of human improvement." – Dugold Stewart.

As mentioned earlier, creative imagination is in all of us, not just poets and inventors. Our brain and nervous system (our subconscious mind) work with our creative imagination as a goal-striving mechanism that operates automatically to achieve any goal we set before it, automatically making course corrections as needed, similar to the way a self-guided torpedo operates.

According to the research of John Bargh and Ezequiel Morsella; "Over the past 30 years, there has been much research on the extent to which people are aware of the important influences on their judgments and decisions and of the reasons for their behavior. This research, in contrast with the cognitive psychology tradition, has led to the view that the *unconscious mind* is a pervasive, powerful influence over such higher mental processes."

Consistent with these basic assumptions in natural science, social cognition research over the past 25 years has produced a stream of surprising findings regarding complex judgmental and behavioral phenomena that operate outside of our awareness. When placed in the broader context of the natural sciences, especially evolutionary biology, the widespread discoveries of sophisticated subconscious behavior guidance systems not only make sense, they turn out to have been predicted on scientific grounds.

Supporting Research

These recent studies have now shown that subconscious goal pursuit produces the same outcomes that conscious goal pursuit does (Google - Dijksterhuis, Chartrand, & Aarts, 2007, and Fitzsimons & Bargh, 2004). The goal concept, once activated without the participant's awareness, operates over extended periods of time *without the person's conscious involvement* to guide thought or behavior towards the goal (Google - Bargh, Gollwitzer, Lee-Chai, & Troetschel, 2001).

The idea that action precedes manifestation is not new. Several theorists have suggested that the conscious mind is not the source or origin of our behavior. It is understood that impulses to act are subconsciously activated and that the role of consciousness is as gatekeeper and sense maker after the fact. In this model, conscious processes kick in after a behavioral impulse has occurred in the brain. In plain language, the impulse is first generated unconsciously, and then consciousness experiences it as its own. (Google - Gazzaniga, 1985; James, 1890; Libet, 1986; Wegner, 2002).

Given the research reviewed above, there is conclusive scientific evidence that behavioral impulses are generated by our subconscious motives, personal preferences, cultural norms, values, and past experiences. In other words, there is no shortage of suggestions from our subconscious as to what to do in any given situation.

It's Nature *and* Nurture

According to Dr. Maltz, "we could relieve ourselves of a vast load of care, anxiety, and worry, if we would recognize that our Creator designed us to live successfully by providing us with a built-in automatic creative mechanism." For some, at least at first, it can be a struggle to let their creative mechanism work and not try to solve problems through conscious effort or "forebrain thinking."

The human forebrain is comparable to the "operator" of an electronic brain or any other type of servomechanism. We use our forebrain when we think about our sense of identity, use our imagination or set goals.

We also use it to gather information, make observations, and evaluate incoming sensory data. But the forebrain cannot create. It is designed to pose problems, but it cannot solve them.

Most people wrongly attribute the need to consciously solve problems to human nature. It is a learned expectation. Jesus said that a man cannot add one cubit to his stature by "taking thought." The reality of the matter is that we cannot even pick up a pencil solely by conscious thought. Without detailed information on human musculoskeletal motor functions, one would be hard pressed to perform the simple task without some assistance from stored memory of picking up pencils. Because we believe we depend almost entirely on our fore brain thinking and deliberate thoughts, we fear failure of the simplest tasks.

This tendency to consciously create and control results is, over time, detrimental to humans. William James suggests that we "confine our conscious efforts to making general resolutions and setting long-term goals, then let the details work themselves out." James goes on to say, "Once a decision is reached and execution is the order of the day, dismiss all responsibility and care about the outcome. Unclamp, in a word, your intellectual and practical machinery and let it run free; and the service it will do you will be twice as good."

Recorded history is replete with examples of how the creative mechanism has delivered answers to life's questions and ideas exactly when needed but only after someone stopped, or took a break from, trying to "think" up the answer or idea. This process of consciously thinking through an idea then letting our creative mechanism bring it to fruition is not reserved for writers, inventors, and artists.

We all have a creative mechanism. Whether you are a schoolteacher, a fulltime parent, student, salesperson, or businessperson, your creative imagination has helped you realize ideas you thought about at some point. Put another way, we all have the same "success mechanism" within us that works to solve personal problems, run a business, or sell products and services, just as it does to write a book, paint a picture, or invent the next gizmo that helps manufacture better widgets.

Developing Skills Naturally

The success mechanism with you can work the same way to produce creative behavior the same way it produces creative ideas. Skill in any area, whether it be sales, playing an instrument, or having a conversation, is not developed by consciously thinking through each action as it is performed. Creative performance is meant to be relaxed, spontaneous, and natural as opposed to self-conscious and analyzed.

Concert pianists could hardly play any composition if they tried to consciously think out which finger should strike which key while they were playing. In reality, they give conscious thought to form and specifics when learning the correct behavior, then practicing the appropriate motions or behavior until it becomes natural and subconscious.

When we are too concerned with how to do something, it has the effect of blocking our creative mechanism similar to the way wireless signals are distorted when there are too many signals in the same area. Our creative mechanism has to sort through the "thought congestion" to decipher our goals.

One reason many people are self-conscious in social situations is that they are trying to consciously control how they interact, what they say, and how others might perceive them. This scenario plays out everywhere from social gatherings, high schools, college campuses, and the workplace. If people would stop trying to be or act the way they think other people expect them to be or act, they could easily be more creative and spontaneous and generally just be themselves.

There are literally thousands of books, blogs, and articles on what I would summarize as "how to stop worrying and start living." To list them here would turn this short book into a multi-volume box set. Just to read them all and rank them according to the various self-improvement principles would likely take decades. So here are just five of the tried and true guidelines for freeing your creative mechanism and learning to trust those hunches and feelings that come from your subconscious mind.

Do the thinking, sorting through options, and planning, prior to deciding. Once you have decided, move on to something else. Many great ideas have been undermined by second and third guessing a decision and trying to consciously direct the outcome. That is not to say take the "let the chips falls where they may" approach. As a course of action reveals new details or variables, your creative mechanism will incorporate them and adjust your course appropriately to move you toward your desired outcome.

Next, Develop the habit of living in the present. Your creative mechanism cannot function in the future. It will only work on today, your current environment. Make plans for tomorrow and set long-range goals. But live in the present. Don't try and live in tomorrow or in the past. Develop the habit of responding to the present moment. Your creative mechanism can respond appropriately and successfully to your present environment only if you are focused on the present and accurately give it input from your present environment. It cannot respond to what may happen tomorrow, until tomorrow becomes today.

Third, try and do only one thing at a time. Multi-tasking may seem efficient and productive. It is all too common these days to be watching television, texting, and perusing Facebook simultaneously. Project managers are routinely expected to keep management updated on current jobs while simultaneously forecasting future projected revenue and billing completed projects in a timely manner. Then, there the people who text or video chat, and read and send emails while driving 60 mph in traffic.

This modern trend is particularly deceptive because it is a major source of stress, hurriedness, and anxiety, but is seldom recognized for what it is. When we consider all the things we "need" to get done in a typical day, anxiety starts to creep in, and escalates with every delay or unforeseen obstacle. The anxiety and worry are not caused by the number of tasks we have to do. It is caused by our "belief" that we should be able to do several things simultaneously.

The truth is, while we can be thinking about several things at any given moment, we can only "do" one thing at a time. Realizing this fact and learning to believe this simple and logical truth enables us to mentally stop trying to do the next task and focus our conscious awareness on what we are doing now. This methodical approach allows us to relax, not feel rushed or anxious, and think clearly about the task at hand thereby performing at our best.

Fourth, take a break. Some decisions simply require a lot of thought and planning. Others require many details to be considered before a course of action can be decided. Still others, such as engineering calculations require a person to remember and apply a lengthy or complex protocol or methodology in order to select the correct equipment for a specific application. Whatever the circumstance, sometimes we just need to lay out all the pieces and take a break or sleep on it.

Remember that your creative mechanism works best when there is not too much interference from your conscious thoughts. Your subconscious mind works even while you sleep to carry out the instructions and expectations you consciously place on it, as long as those expectations are based on truth and strong desire.

There is an old fairytale about a cobbler who found that if he cut out the leather pieces and layout the pattern before retiring for the day, elves would come in while he slept and put the shoes together. The point being, rather than worrying about getting everything finished every day, sometimes you can be more productive by just planning your goals, consciously putting what you need in place, then letting your creative mechanism work out how everything comes together to accomplish the task you assigned to it.

Even yours truly has used this technique since learning about cybernetics and how to program my creative servomechanism in the late 1980's. The very words you are reading, for the most part, are the result of the same process. I have a set goal to write 1,500 to 2000 words each day until I complete a chapter, a blog article, or work all the way through a topic I've chosen to write about.

Since I have other interests throughout the day and evening, sometimes I simply string together relevant thoughts in my mind while doing other things so my creative mechanism can develop the story. At the end of a typical day I like to write down a heading or chapter title for the next day. Then, while relaxing, I think about things or read an article or book related to my chosen topic before I go to sleep. During the night, I know that my subconscious mind will continue to work on what I put into it just before going to sleep. I generally wake up the next morning with plenty to write about.

Fifth, relax while you work. There will always be things that must be done. Some tasks have deadlines, other people may be waiting for you to complete a task, arrive for a meeting, prepare a report, cook a meal, do laundry, or any number of other things. While you go about your daily activities, remember that you matter. You are important and your wellbeing is your responsibility. Throughout your day, periodically take a moment to relax and remember that you matter.

Practical Application: Practice remembering to relax several times each day. You may be surprised how much it reduces mental and physical fatigue, and how much better you can handle the many demands made of you daily. By remembering to take a moment to relax now and then, you will remove many of the stressors and anxiety producing thoughts that interfere with the efficient operation of your creative mechanism.

What are the key points from this chapter you want to remember?

Chapter 6

Happiness is a Learned Habit

"Most people are about as happy as they make up their minds to be." – Abraham Lincoln

Ask someone what they want in life and chances are they'll say something along the lines of "I just want to be happy." When you ask them why they aren't happy, they can usually point out the causes of their discontent immediately; They work too much, make too little money, don't feel motivated, are unhappy in their job, or something along those lines.

We often think of "happiness" as cheerfulness or the kind of pleasure that comes from instant gratification. Greek thinker Aristippus the Elder, called this perspective "Hedonic happiness" and suggested we should seek as much pleasure as possible and generally avoid as much pain as possible. One can see how this approach leads to a slippery slope. Addiction, in all its forms – from alcohol to shopping, gambling to Facebook scrolling – is fed by the dopamine rush of these pleasure inputs.

But there is another kind of happiness that derives from deep satisfaction and fulfillment – a deep delight with all of life – that is especially relevant to new habit formation. While this delight is more enduring than the temporary pleasures of cold ice cream on a summer day or the thrill of driving a new car, it doesn't always feel good.

To lead a more fulfilling life, we can think of happiness as a skill to be cultivated or a practice to be learned, a practice shaped by the rewarding virtues and habits of character you wish to embody. This conception of happiness is based on the understanding that pleasure and amusement are meant to serve our ideals, to rejuvenate us so that we may pursue worthy goals.

According to Dr. Maxwell Maltz, "Happiness is not something that is earned or deserved." And that, "Happiness is simply a state of mind in which our thinking is pleasant a good share of the time." Many times, it is not what happens in our lives that makes us unhappy, but our opinion of what happens. Just because it rains on the only day you could play golf doesn't make it a bad day. Nor does it mean mother nature is out to ruin your life. It just means it's a rainy day.

When a former employer had to sell his business he said to me, "With the discovery of a software programming error, I just lost $170,000. I've lost everything and have become a disgrace to my family. When I suggested he not make things worse by adding his opinion to the facts, he said perhaps I didn't hear him correctly. I responded that it was a "fact" that a software programming error resulted in a $170,000 shortfall and the probable loss of his business. But it was only his "opinion" that he had lost "everything" and became a disgrace to his family.

Many people do not pursue happiness because they have been taught that it is selfish, sinful, or wrong. But those teachings are wrong. However, one of the most pleasant feelings human beings experience is of being needed and wanted by another human being. It lets a person know they are important, perceived as competent, and that they contribute to the happiness of another person. This kind of happiness encourages unselfishness and service toward others. However, if we make happiness a moral issue and something to be earned as a reward for unselfish acts, then we are indeed apt to feel guilty for seeking happiness.

Learning the Happiness Habit

According to Dr. Matthew Chappell, "Happiness is produced internally, not by objects, but by ideas, thoughts, and attitudes which can be developed and constructed by the individual's own activities, irrespective of their environment."

The human brain is wired (and re-wired) through positive and negative reinforcement. Habits form as we learn to identify cues tied to specific rewards and then exhibit a specific behavior to obtain that reward. For a basic example, you see a favorite food, eat that food, and dopamine floods your brain making you feel good. Conversely, trouble arises when we transpose triggers for the same reward. Basically, you learn to associate food with feeling good and may find yourself stress eating for the emotional reward rather than satisfying a physical need. Thus a "bad habit" is established.

Generally speaking, we react to petty annoyances and frustrations with irritability, dissatisfaction, or resentment purely out of habit. We have practiced responding that way to similar events that it has become habitual. Most of these habitual unhappiness responses originated with some event which was interpreted as an insult to our self-esteem. Maybe another driver honks at us when we are just as stuck in traffic as they are; maybe you planned to play golf after a busy week, and it rains that day, at your tee time. Whatever the cause, we react with anger, resentment, self-pity, in other words unhappiness.

Have you ever caught a behind-the-scenes camera shot of a talk show or game show? An assistant off camera holds up a sign telling the audience when to applaud, when to laugh, etc. The audience are controlled like sheep and respond as they are directed to. It is the same principle when we let external events and other people dictate how we should feel or react in a given situation. This is a learned behavior.

Robert Louis Stevenson said, "The habit of being happy enables one to be freed, or largely freed, from the domination of external conditions." Regaining subconscious control over this habit involves a degree of mindfulness. Mindfulness is a practice of switching your attention from reacting to a given stimuli to heightening your awareness of your thoughts as they arise.

We often develop bad habits unconsciously, but it takes conscious effort to change them or form desirable ones. It is difficult to maintain this conscious effort because most of the time we resolve to give up something that brought us comfort, or we resolve to show more self-discipline. In short, breaking undesired habits and starting desired habits is hard and usually somewhat unpleasant. So, what if we replaced "discipline" with more "delight" and character development as a motivator?

By shifting your attention from frustration or resentment to curiosity, you can learn to see your situation and emotions from a more objective perspective. But trying to develop a "mindfulness habit" alone is not enough to help most people reverse an undesirable habit. What is the desired character outcome you want from a new habit? How will that desired outcome replace the perceived pleasure you felt from the undesired habit?

As a behavior becomes a habit, it is programmed into our servo-mechanism and becomes an automatic response, requiring little if any conscious thought. This is because the neural pathways in our brains actually change as routine behaviors are paired with deeply held beliefs. It is scientifically established that the circuitry of the brain changes as repeated thoughts and behaviors create engrams in the long-term memory areas of the brain.

Rewiring Your Brain

Whether you want to be successful as an entrepreneur or just in trimming your waistline, the strategies are the same. Your success is ultimately determined by the decisions you make daily, otherwise known as your habits.

If you set goals that aren't important to you, you aren't likely to achieve them. Make sure you are truly passionate about the goals you set. Focus on only a few at a time. While it's great to have a list of goals, you can have more success if you concentrate your energy toward one or two at a time.

Describe your goals with detailed specifics so your creative mechanism will have a clear and detailed objective. Vague goals mean vague results. After you have identified your top goals, write down in detail why it's important for you to achieve each one. Getting started is often where many people get stuck, so make sure to tap into the emotional tone of each goal, to push you into action. And don't forget: The difference between a dream and a goal is a deadline.

Let's say you decide you set a goal to work out 20 minutes each day. Now imagine if you only worked out on days when you woke up feeling rested, and in a happy mood. If your workouts are dependent upon you being in a joyous state, they aren't likely to happen regularly. Decide the actions you are going to take and follow through despite your mood. When you exercise when you don't feel like it, you are working out your discipline muscle too. You will be proud of keeping your commitments. This same mentality works for any goal. If you are starting your website for your new small business and tackle projects you dread, you will build up your discipline. Remember, it won't actually be easier tomorrow unless you do it today. Whenever you feel like quitting, think about why you started in the first place.

Be Consistent

Generally speaking, no one has to remind us to go to bed at night or brush our teeth because those behaviors have become habits developed over time. What other automatic habits do you maintain? Maybe every morning you take an hour and research a new social media strategy to promote your new business. Come up with habits that support your goals and make them automatic so you can make daily, consistent progress. Persistence supersedes talent, genetics and luck. There can be no true success without consistent practice of success habits.

When you set your goals, identify benchmarks to assess how you are doing. It's easy to be excited about a new goal in the beginning, but your results depend on the actions you take each day. At the start of a new month, see how you are doing. What is working? What isn't? Determine how to do more of what's working to expedite your progress. When you regularly track your progress, you develop the discipline to stay connected to your goals.

One reason people give up on their goals is because they tend to look at how far they still have to go, instead of recognizing the progress they have already made. Another reason is the lack of an example or role model. Has someone else successfully achieved what you want to achieve? Research the success habits of others and incorporate those habits into your own life. The fastest way to achieve your goals is by developing the habits of success!

Our self-image and our habits tend to go together. Changing a habit will automatically change your self-image. Habits are simply learned, automatic reactions and responses we perform without much conscious thought. They are behaviors we have programmed into our creative mechanism. When we consciously and deliberately develop new and better habits, our self-image tends to "outgrow" our old habits and grow into the new behavior patterns.

Practical Application: For the next 30 days, start each day with this statement: "I am beginning my day in a better way." Then, throughout the day, consciously decide that:

I will be as cheerful as possible.

I will attempt to feel and act more friendly toward other people.

I am going to be a little less critical and a little more tolerant of other people and will place the best possible interpretation on the actions.

My success is inevitable. I will consciously act and feel like the success I want to be.

I will not let my opinion color facts in a negative or pessimistic way.

Regardless of what happens, I will react calmly and intelligently.

Key points from this chapter:

Chapter 7

Developing Successful Personality Traits

The first thing anyone wanting to develop successful personality traits must do is identify exactly what a successful personality looks like. Remember, the automatic goal striving servomechanism inside you must have a clear, unambiguous goal or target to shoot for. Many well-intended people start down the road of building a better self-image but fail to have a clearly defined image of what they seek to accomplish or a clear sense of direction.

Successful people know that the strength of their personality is based on their ability to understand and adapt to changing circumstances and to know how and when to seize on opportunities amid changing environments. Understanding how your personality affects various environments, and vice versa, will fuel your desire to constantly learn and grow. Learning and adaptability hinges on developing critical thinking skills, accepting uncertainty, having social and emotional intelligence, and always having the desire and determination to push forward.

Successful personalities know when to talk and when to listen. They are effective communicators and are able to explain clearly and succinctly everything from organizational goals to specific tasks. If people don't understand or aren't aware of your expectations, they will fall short, so the more specific you can be, the better. You need to be able to communicate on all levels: one on one, to management, in person, as well as via phone, email and social media. Communication is built on a steady flow of verbal and nonverbal exchanges of ideas and information, so work on being approachable and involving people from different levels.

To be sure, having a clearly defined goal and understanding of your environment will not be enough. Successful personalities also have the courage to act. Admiral William F. Halsey said, "The best defense is a strong offense, but its application is wider than war." All challenges, whether personal, professional, economic, or political, become smaller if you confront them instead of avoiding them.

Successful personalities must have the courage to risk innovation and encourage creativity in others. Doing this will foster the creativity that will steer you to new destinations and around the twists and turns of changing environments. The courage to act in tough circumstances requires faith in yourself. After all, faith is not about believing something in spite of the evidence. It is the courage to do something regardless of the consequences.

It is as important to address the underlying aspect of one's personality as it is to develop successful behaviors. One variable seldom mentioned in the professional development and self-help literature is that of the self-esteem. Carlyle once said, "Alas, fearful unbelief is unbelief in yourself." Of all the pitfalls in life, a broken self-esteem is perhaps the most difficult to overcome because it is a pit dug by our own hands.

The costs of surrendering to defeatism, the cause of low self-esteem, is high, both to the individual in terms of material gains and personal achievements lost and to others via strained relationships. The quote from Carlyle was likely his acknowledgment of his own obnoxious personality and appalling domestic tyranny.

Of course, Carlyle was an extreme case, but nonetheless indicative of the typical mindset when we most doubt ourselves and our ability to overcome adversity. That is usually when we are the most difficult to get along with. Holding a low perception of ourselves is a vice, not a virtue. When we first begin a significant undertaking, we may not start with a great deal of confidence in our ability to see it through. Confidence is gained through experiencing successful outcomes. Whether it is riding a bicycle, speaking in public, raising children, or performing brain surgery, success breeds success. It works exactly the same when building self-confidence.

One of the easiest ways to build your self-confidence is through a series of graduated successes. This means learning to prioritize your goals and being responsible for accomplishing those objectives before tackling larger ones.

It is important to form the habit of remembering past successes and forgetting failures. This is the way your internal success mechanism works and how you learn to succeed. The reason past failures readily come to mind is because they are usually accompanied by an emotional response. When you experience success, it is okay to enjoy an emotional response as well. Over time, your self-confidence will grow as you experience more and more success, learn to regulate your time, attention and emotions, hold yourself accountable and learn from your mistakes.

Another significant trait of a successful personality has a great deal to do with a person's self-image. According to Dr. Maltz in *Psycho-Cybernetics*, "No real success or genuine happiness is possible until a person gains some degree of self-acceptance. There is often a sense of relief when someone who has been trying to be everything they think other people expect them to be decides to just be themselves.

Changing your self-image does not mean changing who you are. It means changing the mental picture of yourself that you hold in your mind. Developing a realistic self-image is more about self-realization and self-revelation than transformation. You, your "self" is what it was created to be. You did not create it, and you cannot change it. You can, however, realize it, and make the most of who you are by accepting a true perception of your real self.

You matter, not because of where you live, what kind car you drive, how much money you make, or any other external influence. You matter because you are devinely designed in the image of your Creator. Most people are better, stronger, wiser, and more competent than they realize. Creating a better self-image does not *create* new abilities or talents, it releases them. While we cannot change our basic self, we can change our personality. Personality is a tool of sorts, an image of ourselves we use to interact with our environment and the world. It is the sum total of our habits, attitudes, and skills we have learned to use to express who we want others to believe we are.

We Make Mistakes, They Don't Make Us

Accepting who we are, just as we are, is easier when we realize that even though we *make* mistakes, we *are not* mistakes. You do not have to be defined by your past or mistakes. But you must recognize them in order to correct them and learn from them. Recognition is the starting place for any significant life change. The first step in acquiring knowledge is recognizing that we are unaware of or uninformed about something. The first step in salvation is recognizing we have sinned. The first step in getting stronger is recognizing we are weak in some aspect.

The process of creating a successful self-image involves using the negative feedback from our past mistakes to make course corrections. Throughout our lives it is in our nature to move toward self-improvement. This path is more difficult to travel when one attempts to carry the excess baggage of a fictitious self-perception. Besides the significant mental strain, trying to maintain false perceptions invites continuous frustration and disappointment when trying to operate in the real world with a fictitious self-image.

Learning to emotionally tolerate imperfections in oneself can be difficult for some people. However, it is necessary to recognize our shortcomings in order to use that knowledge to improve our self-image and behavior. You are not a bad person just because you made a mistake. Nor are you a good person just because do something good. My grandfather used to say that "going to church doesn't make you a

Christian any more than working in a hen house makes you a chicken." You must be able to differentiate between YOU and your behavior.

The Power of Words

It is so easy for us to tell a child they are bad or naughty for doing a something wrong. It is also easy for us to say to another person they are useless or lazy because they don't do what we expected of them or for breaking social norms. It may be that your parents or teachers said something like this to you and up to now it has been the only way that you have known to behave.

One of the reasons we should choose our words carefully is when we say things to someone, that person may develop a limiting belief about themself, which can affect their life long term. Think of a small child who has done something the parent disapproves of. Then the parent says to that child, "you will never amount to anything, you are useless and lazy. You are stupid."

These and so many other statements have caused many to grow up believing these things about themselves and as they get older, they don't strive for being better or doing something different because they remember those words. They may have been spoken in anger or frustration and not meant, but the damage is already done.

Two of the foundational presuppositions employed by the management at Riggs Consulting in Houston, Texas, a life-skills and management coaching firm, is that "people are not their behavior," and that "people can change their behaviors, and thereby their self-perception." This is great news for most people. You are not your behavior. You can learn and reprogram your success mechanism to follow new strategies.

Even if you have only known the ways of shouting and cursing, the fact that people are not their behaviors means you can change your behavior. It also means you can be the person YOU want to be. By differentiating your self-image from your behavior, you empower yourself to breaking free from other's perceptions of your previous behavior and be the person you want to be.

In fact, as you learn and apply these truths, you can teach others that behavior is something we do, not who we are as people. The more you empower other people, the better you will feel about yourself and the better you feel about yourself the more you will do that for others.

Practical Application: Take few minutes and write down 4-5 examples of how you have been taught to believe something about yourself that was originally based on a behavior or opinion rather than your real self, and what you will do to change that perception.

Chapter 8

Reframing Negative Self-Perceptions

As we go about our daily lives we are constantly thinking about and interpreting the environments we find ourselves in. Our subconscious act as an internal voice inside our head that determines how we perceive every situation. Psychologists call this inner voice "self-talk" and it includes our conscious thoughts as well as our unconscious assumptions or beliefs. These deeply held beliefs make up our self-perception.

If your current self-perception is not serving you in ways that allow you to be your best self and achieve the goals you're aiming for, it's time to reframe the underlying beliefs and reprogram your automatic success mechanism. Your self-perception is about the relationship you have with *yourself.* The good news is that because you created this self-perception, you are the person most capable of transforming it.

No one just decides one day to develop a list of negative personality traits. They don't just show up one day either. Nor do they reveal a fallen human nature. Also, no one is immune to negative thoughts and feelings. Celebrities, politicians, and most everyone else, at one time or another, experiences this sort of negative feedback. What matters is that you recognize them for what they are and take positive action to correct your course.

Research has shown that childhood and the sometime awkward years of adolescence are common sources of many harmful self-perceptions we develop as adults. Now, as adults, we can see how and why we came to think about ourselves in the ways we do. Old engrams from our inner critic seek to remind us of our unworthiness or inadequacy and work to suppress any excitement and hope you had of achieving your goals with questions like: "Who are you to think you can do this? Who are you to think you even deserve this?"

These reminders are not always obvious. Many times, negative feedback comes from seemingly "constructive criticism" or are buried in someone's comment at a social gathering. Think of the friend at dinner who dominates the conversation and commonly speaks over others yet tells you you're rude when you interrupt them. Or, how about the co-worker who claims to be a perfectionist but always struggles to meet deadlines, then says your work will never be as good as theirs because you prioritize meeting deadlines over doing better quality work.

When you are on the receiving end of sharp, unsavory criticism, there's a good chance the other person may also be projecting their own self-perception on you. Thereby unwittingly showing you how they see the world and the flaws they see in themselves.

Projections are often an unconscious way people defend themselves to feel better emotionally and mentally about those aspects of their "self" they consider to be flawed. Sometimes, we attribute the things we don't like about ourselves to someone else because the pain and discomfort of confessing our own inadequacies are just too great. However, simply cutting ties with anyone whose negative opinions leave you feeling you are a lesser human being would lead to an incredibly lonely existence. What may better serve you is recognizing when someone might actually be projecting their self-image upon you. Everyone is entitled to their own opinion. Whether you adopt it as your own, as a truth about you, is your choice and no one else's.

Controlling Resentment

It is difficult to not resent someone's derogatory comment or opinion, regardless how subtly spoken, especially when it's made in a public setting such as a restaurant, a conference room or call, or in front of your spouse and children. Still, resentment even when base on real injustices is not the way to win. Resentment is an emotion that sooths our feelings of being victimized. Holding on to resentment becomes a habitual response to similar events and contributes to sense of victimhood.

Habitual resentment eventually leads to self-pity, one of the worst emotional habits one can develop, and contributes significantly to an inferior self-image. It is important to remember here that resentment is not caused by another person's comment, events, or circumstances. It is caused by your own reaction and emotional response to those comments, events, or circumstances.

Because of its emotional moorings, as long as you harbor resentment, it will be difficult, if not impossible, for you to see yourself as a self-reliant, self-confident, person. Resentment is therefore inconsistent with the creative, goal striving mechanism. Remember, in creative goal striving, you are the active determinant of your own truth, not a passive depository of other people's opinions.

How Others Contribute to Our Self-Perception

Once you start looking at your personality and behavior as a reflection of your self-image, you may be surprised by how much of your thinking is inaccurate, exaggerated, or focused on the opinions of others. One of the most common mistakes we make is to confuse our behavior with our "self" and conclude that because we did something, an act, it now defines who we are, a state of being.

To say, "I failed," is to recognize *you made a mistake* that can be corrected. However, to say, "I am a failure," is to assume *the mistake made you*. This false assumption, or negative self-talk, reinforces the mistake and makes it a permanent part of yourself-perception. To use a basic illustration, when watching a child learning to walk, we know they are going to fall, and we say, "she was trying to walk, and she fell." We do not conclude, "she is a faller."

Conversely, many parents, teachers, and others fail to apply the same reasoning when listening to a child learning to talk. As children are learning to pronoun words and string them together to form a sentence or question, because they are consciously trying to remember and speak correctly, they often hesitate and repeat parts of words. Naturally concerned parents prematurely conclude; "He is a stutterer." This is a judgement of the child, rather than an assessment his actions at the moment. According to speech pathologist Dr. Wendell Johnson, this judgement from parents or teachers, individuals children regard as "all knowing," is taken to heart. The child now identifies himself as a stutterer, and the impediment typically becomes permanent.

Another study conducted by Dr. Knight Dunlap over a twenty year period revealed that a key distinction between non-stutterers and stutterers was the way parents, teachers, and other listeners, not familiar with normal speech development, described the children. The parents of children who did not stutter typically used descriptive terminology such as, "She *did not* speak ...," when discussing their child learning to speak. While parents of children who stuttered typically used judgmental terms such as, "He *could not* speak ...," to describe their child learning to speak.

Dr. Dunlap also stated that in case after case, it was determined that the subjects, children, in fact did not have a speech impediment. Typically, the impediment was "assumed" after parents and other listeners concluded and convinced the children who stuttered that "they could not speak properly." Dr. Dunlap also concluded that the same learning principle applied to virtually all bad habits. It is essential, said Dr. Dunlap, that the person learn to stop blaming himself and condemning himself regarding his habits if he is to correct his behavior.

Repurposing Negative Self-Talk

Regardless of the source of our personal beliefs, they all were formed in response to how we perceived the events in our past. While each of our beliefs serves a different purpose, when combined with our self-talk, they generally support a common goal: to protect us and keep us safe from perceived threats, whether real or imagined.

The more we learn about how and why our beliefs were formed, the better we can evaluate whether those beliefs are still valid. If we find a particular negative response is inconsistent with our desired self-image, we can now repurpose them to our advantage to help us get to where we want to go.

You don't need to undergo intensive therapy to benefit from some simple language re-framing techniques. When you change a few words in your self-image narrative, you can drastically change the impact that narrative can have on you. First, let's start with a general question. Ask yourself, "Does how I see myself make me feel better or worse about myself?" Or, if you want to get more specific, "Does how I see myself create obstacles between where I am, what I am feeling, where I want to be, and how I want to feel about myself?"

Consider the statement; "No one loves me. I'm not attractive." You can get a sense of how negative self-talk, as a statement of fact, reinforces a belief? Now, let's re-purpose that belief to say, "Right now, I feel like no one loves me, and I don't feel attractive." See how reframing the statement leaves the belief open to change?

Many times, our self-perceptions tend to be purely black and white. Meaning we tend to think in terms of absolute facts rather than our interpretations of those facts. We also tend to inaccurately and blanketly apply them to cover all contexts and situations, particularly when our emotions are the most intense. Reframing your self-narrative is easier than trying to eliminate it and start over. Recognize that your self-perception is only a reflection of the emotions you are feeling at particular moments in time and you'll become better at preserving your self-image.

However, no amount of reframed self-talk can transform negative self-perceptions if you do not believe the old perception is no longer true. In the previous example, the repurposed belief and self-talk might sound something like, "I used to think no one loved me, because I didn't feel attractive. But I now understand that I am loved for who I am, and that helps me feel attractive."

Notice how there is no mention of looking to improve or delete an aspect of your personality in either of these statements? Also, notice the absence of the word "improve." Using the word improve, could imply there is something wrong with you, to begin with. You're changing your *perception* of you. You do not need to change you. Your subconscious will be more on board with you using the phrasing above because you're emotionally more receptive to it. It *feels* safe. It *feels* honest. It *feels* true.

With practice, you can learn to notice your own negative self-talk as it happens, and consciously choose to think about the situation in a more realistic and helpful way. Repurposing your self-talk means challenging the validity of negative aspects of your personality. Doing this enables you to feel better and to respond to situations in a more helpful way. Learning to reframe negative thoughts might take time and practice but is worth the effort.

When you engage your creative mechanism, you can change behavioral and emotional responses that signal to your brain what you are focusing on is important. The more you refine the details in which you paint a healthier and helpful self-perception, the more your servomechanism will look for opportunities for this to come to fruition in reality. From recognizing our negative self-perceptions, we can start to shape those which aren't just healthier for us but also strategically helpful for us in moving toward the life we want to experience.

Practical Application: Whenever you find yourself feeling depressed, angry, anxious or upset, use this as your signal to stop and become aware of your thoughts. Use your feelings as your cue to reflect on your thinking. A good way to test the accuracy of your perceptions might be to ask yourself the following questions and write down your thoughts. These questions will help you to check out your self-talk to see whether your current view is reasonable. This will also help you discover other ways of thinking about your self-image.

What is my evidence for and against my thinking?

Are my beliefs based on fact or opinion?

Do I jump to negative conclusions?

If I were being positive, how would I perceive myself?

Is this situation as bad as I am making out to be?

Chapter 9

Attaining Peace of Mind

"The life of inner peace, being harmonious and without stress, is the easiest type of existence."

- Norman Vincent Peale

The mind is most useful and efficient when you are able to accept or reject thoughts at will, and not be distracted by every thought that passes through your mind. It is understood that our minds are always busy, always thinking, but many of our daily thoughts are not really useful or necessary to us personally. I am mainly referring to negative thoughts, worries and fears. Most people are seemingly enslaved by external stimuli and "feel" a need to respond automatically. It does not even occur to them that they can become free from this mindless obedience at will.

Reducing Mental Clutter

If you follow every thought that enters your mind your attention spam would be close to zero. The habit of constantly thinking is very deeply ingrained in the human mind, but even this habit can be modified. It would be a great advantage if you were able to eliminate some of the clutter when you want to and, with a little training, you will be able to choose to ignore distracting thoughts when you want to. When there are fewer thoughts demanding your attention, you enjoy inner peace and happiness.

With this state of mind, you will be able to do everything in a better, and more focused and efficient manner. By learning to reduce the number of thoughts in your mind, you attain mastery over your mind, and become able to focus it on whatever you want.

Let's look at a common experience. Suppose you are sitting in your favorite chair and enjoying reading this book. Suddenly your cell phone rings. Without thinking or making a conscious decision to answer it, you automatically reach for, or get up and go get your phone. From experience and out of habit, you recognize a ringtone as a stimulus you have learned to "obey."

You were all set to spend an hour relaxing and reading, but your automatic response mechanism has moved you out of your relaxed state due to an external stimuli it has been conditioned to respond to. The point being you do not *have to* answer a ringing phone. You do not have to obey every thought. You can simply *choose to* stay relaxed and continue reading by consciously deciding to not respond to the distraction.

I recently, as in the past year, have experimented with this exact re-conditioning described above. There are a few things we can do today that were not an option twenty plus years ago. Unlike the days of telephone landlines, most people today have, or have access to, a cell phone. Twenty years ago, standard home phones had an actual bell in them that rang obnoxiously loud when someone called. Today, ringtones may or may not jar us out of concentration or startle us during a movie, but they still elicit the same automatic response.

For many years I carried two phones, one for work and one for personal calls. About a year ago, since most of the calls to my personal phone were telemarketers, I decided to stop carrying my personal phone when I was at work and I stopped carrying my work phone on the weekends. This "untethering" felt great and gave me a sense of control over my time and limited others' access to me, with the exception of family of course.

I began to realize that my staff and coworkers got along fine without me over the weekends. In fact, they wondered aloud why I kept my work phone on me when away from the office to begin with. If my wife and family needed to reach me during the day, they knew I was always at work, so they usually called that number anyway. Deciding to not answer the phone was liberating.

After many years of thinking "I need to be accessible 24/7 in case someone needed something," I found that what I really needed was downtime to relax and recharge. Because I have been a student and practitioner of cybernetics since 1986, I knew that meant I had to consciously decide to disconnect from all non-essential external stimuli and consciously decide whether or not to let something or someone disturb my family-time and weekends.

Conditioning vs Self-Control

In much the same way you automatically obey or respond to a ringing telephone, you also become conditioned to respond in specific ways to various stimuli in your environment. Many theorists liken this automatic response to classical conditioning when it is perhaps better explained by operant conditioning.

For those not familiar with Russian physiologist Ivan Pavlov's experiment where he "conditioned" a dog to salivate at the sound of a bell, let me explain. The field of behavioral psychology uses the terms *Classical Conditioning* and *Operant Conditioning* to identify the process whereby human beings are trained to respond a certain way to a given stimulus.

In clinical jargon, Classical Conditioning involves pairing a previously neutral stimulus, such as the sound of a bell, with an unconditioned stimulus such as the taste of food. In Pavlov's experiment, he would ring a bell and then present the dog with food. Soon, the dog would salivate at the sound of the bell whether the food was present or not. The sound of the bell is known as the conditioned stimulus, and salivating, the response to the bell, is known as the conditioned response.

Classical conditioning is much more than just a basic term used to describe a method of learning; it can also explain how a bad habit might form. For example, you have been working out regularly and eating healthy, but late night snacking keeps tripping up your weight loss efforts. Thanks to classical conditioning, you might have developed the habit of heading to the kitchen for a snack every time a commercial comes on while you are watching your favorite television program.

While commercial breaks were once a neutral stimulus, repeated pairing with an unconditioned stimulus (having a delicious snack) has turned the commercials into a conditioned stimulus. Now every time you see a commercial, you crave a sweet treat.

Operant conditioning, according to J.E. Dunsmore, focuses on using either reinforcement or punishment to increase or decrease a behavior. Through this process, an association is formed between the behavior and the consequences of that behavior.

Imagine that a trainer is trying to teach a dog to fetch a ball. When the dog successfully chases and picks up the ball, the dog receives praise as a reward. When the animal fails to retrieve the ball, the trainer withholds the praise. Eventually, the dog forms an association between the behavior of fetching the ball and receiving the desired reward.

In addition to being used to train people to engage in new behaviors, operant conditioning can also be used to help people eliminate unwanted ones. Using a system of rewards and punishments, people can learn to overcome bad habits that might have a negative impact on their relationships with others and thereby their own self-image.

For example, imagine that a schoolteacher punishes a student for talking out of turn by not letting the student go outside for recess. As a result, the student's consciously forms an association between the behavior, talking out of turn, and the consequence, not being able to go outside for recess. As a result, his subconscious mind is reprogrammed, and the problematic behavior decreases.

In short classical conditioning involves associating an involuntary response and a stimulus, while operant conditioning is about associating a voluntary behavior and a consequence. In operant conditioning, the learner is also rewarded with incentives, while classical conditioning involves no such enticements. Also, classical conditioning is passive on the part of the learner, while operant conditioning requires the learner to actively participate and perform some type of action in order to be rewarded or punished.

Of course, there is much more to the learning theories discussed above, such as who should decide whether or not a behavior should be changed. But, for the focus of this book, suffice it to say that behavioral responses and subconscious beliefs are learned, and therefore can be un-learned and replaced with more productive responses through a person's exercise of self-control.

Self-control has been defined as the capacity to override an impulse in order to respond appropriately. We use self-control when we eat carrots instead of Krispy Kreme donuts, when we show restraint instead of lash out, and when we pay attention to what someone is saying instead of interrupting them with our opinion.

When you make the decision to better control or change an undesired behavior, or a belief that is no longer valid, it should be based on your own value judgements of the behavior or thinking you wish to change rather than what someone else thinks you should do or believe.

Shaping Beliefs for Peace of Mind

Beliefs are the truths people hold on to and live their lives by. The power of belief can limit you, as in the belief that you deserve only a limited amount of happiness. Or belief can free you, as in the belief that you are capable, accomplished, and valuable. When you consciously evaluate your core beliefs, two things happen. First, you find out who you are, and why you behave the way you do. Second, new energies become available when you pursue the core beliefs that are positive self-image supporting, fulfilling, and spiritually transforming.

As I have mentioned throughout this book, what you believe about yourself has both positive and negative effects. If deep down you sincerely believe, "I can be successful at whatever I put my mind you're your strong desire, sincere belief in your ability, and your creative mechanism will make it happen. However, if you hold this self-perception but believe success involves being ruthless, selfish, and engaging in hurtful behavior, your beliefs literally cannot support your self-image and there will be no peace of mind.

Another peace disrupting tendency humans have that causes worry, anxiety, and insecurity is the bad habit of trying to respond emotionally to potential circumstances or events that have not, and may not, happen, except in our imaginations. Sometimes, to justify our long held beliefs that appear different than our desired self-image, we invent straw men in our imaginations, then emotionally respond to our own perceptions.

In other words, we say things like, "This or that might happen, and I'm not prepared." Then we form negative mental pictures of what *might* exist at some future moment. And finally, we respond emotionally and psychologically to these negative images as if they were our present reality. Remember, your brain and nervous system cannot tell the difference between a real experience and one you vividly imagine.

Managing these types of disturbances to your peace of mind is less a matter of what you choose to do and more a matter of choosing to not do anything. Try and live emotionally in the present moment. Assess your present environment and be aware of what circumstances actually exist in the present and respond to that. Then your responses are likely to be more appropriate and you will have less time to notice or respond to fictitious peace stealing "what ifs."

Practical Application: Unrest and anxiety are most often caused by emotionally over-responding to our environment. You can extinguish old over-response behaviors and thinking. You will need to practice delaying your habitual automatic responses to your environment. Understand that your time and peace of mind are important and under your control. Practice "letting the phone ring" while you continue doing whatever you were doing.

Key points to remember from this chapter:

Chapter 10

Turning Crisis into Creative Opportunity

"The Chinese use two brush strokes to write the word 'crisis.' One brush stroke stands for danger; the other for opportunity. In a crisis, be aware of the danger—but recognize the opportunity."

— John F. Kennedy

Crises come into our lives, no matter how we may try to avoid them. They are troubling, unwanted experiences or events that take us way out of our comfort zone. Typically, crises result in some type of loss. The very nature of a crisis is antithetical to our core values of certainty and predictability.

During a crisis, be it real or manufactured, we need and want to restore order to our lives, even as chaos seems to prevail. Yet, if we learn to reframe how we see crisis, we might actually take advantage of it. There is the potential for transformation as the crisis unfolds into an opportunity, provided we learn to stop resisting unwanted change.

Typically, personal change requires our motivation, imagination and strong desire to serve as the catalyst to power the transformation. Crisis, on the other hand, removes the motivation requirement as it places us squarely outside of our familiar comfort zone. A crisis literally removes the boundaries that define us. We typically find ourselves wanting to get back inside the comfort of a known environment. But there is no going back. And that is where the creative opportunity begins.

What we call crisis is simply the occurrence of change. A crisis is defined in Webster's Dictionary as: "a crucial or decisive point or situation; a turning point." Only when we focus on the phrase "turning point," are we able to turn it into an opportunity.

Are you curious about the unfolding potential of change, or do you focus on the loss of the familiar? Your answer reveals your relationship between loss and opportunity. The former reinforces anxiety and retreat, the latter evokes growth. Steve Jobs might have felt self-defeated and victimized himself after he was fired from Apple many years ago. He chose otherwise.

After his dismissal, Jobs grasped the crisis by the horns, seeing opportunity where others did not. He went on to lead a small animation company and turn it into the juggernaut that is now Pixar. When the Walt Disney Company bought Pixar in 2006, Jobs immediately became the largest shareholder in Disney. The moral of the story is that crisis and unwanted change happens; learn to look beyond it and embrace the temporary discomfort.

Crises tend to present themselves as either acute or chronic circumstances. For example, there is an economic upheaval that is driving the United States and the world economy into highly volatile perturbations, with both wealth and employment literally disappearing. In the lives of most people, this is an external crisis raining upon them, typically not of their own making. Yet, through these losses, many people are coming to reflect on their values and choices and are making adjustments—due to the crisis—that actually benefit them.

A high-powered Wall Street executive had hardly a spare moment for his family, as he was ever consumed with achieving more and more. The loss of his job at first paralyzed him with fear. After a time, however, he was able to reevaluate his priorities. He now works from home in a small business he founded, and he and his family have greatly benefited. Similar stories of economic crisis turned into entrepreneurial opportunity throughout the world now number in the thousands.

Crisis and opportunity are merely different aspects of the transformation process. An unexpected health issue or the death of a loved one may bring anxiety and deep feelings of loss. However painful and stressful these challenges and losses may be, the opportunity to be in the moment and value life from a differing perspective can prevail, if we let it.

The individual whose spouse initiated divorce or left them for another person feels betrayed and perhaps heartsick. After a time, though, they may, in fact, come to feel thankful to be freed from an unworthy and inauthentic relationship. Often, the relationship crisis launches the couple into new territory, whereby growth may finally be achieved. The pain endured through the crisis may actually enable this growth. This is particularly true if they evolve through the loss and benefit from a new and healthier relationship.

I fervently believe that every crisis presents an opportunity. Do you choose to focus on the crisis and freeze in fear, or do you explore the opportunity? Learning to look at the larger themes and patterns that set up these challenges will help develop a vantage point from which you may break through the struggle.

How Crisis Thinking Affects the Mind

Have you ever known someone who was great at something, but would fold under pressure? Many athletes start that way, and some develop themselves through times of crisis, while others allow tough times to limit them. I have watched professional baseball pitchers throw the ball with pinpoint accuracy and blistering speed during the regular season, then get uptight as a high school freshman on prom night when the championship was on the line. There are similar stories from athletes across all sports.

As a university adjunct professor, I witnessed time and again students who performed well on weekly assignments but scored poorly on major examinations. Then, there were students whose attendance and failure to turn in weekly assignments adversely affected their grades but who practically aced the major exams. I leaned heavily on my awareness that everyone is a unique individual with unique learning styles and diverse backgrounds.

Dr. Edward Tolman, while with the University of California, writes, "like most animals, humans form cognitive maps of their environment while they are learning. If the motivation (pressure) is not too intense, these maps are typically broad and general in nature." Meaning that if one path to problem solving is blocked we can approach it from a different angle.

However, Dr. Tolman continues, "if there are crises present (high stakes), the cognitive map will be narrower and more restricted thereby limiting the problem solving to one method, usually learned while getting through a similar crisis in the past. If this one path is blocked, the person becomes frustrated and often fails to recognize other options." With each crisis, this limited perspective becomes fixed. The individual tends to lose the ability to spontaneously react to new situations or improvise.

An interesting example of this phenomenon is the standard fire drill. It has been proven that individuals who have not been trained, through periodic fire escape drills, how to get out of their school or office building, take two to three times as long to exit a building than those who participated in realistic fire drills. The narrow fixated response to the fire bell could save their lives, at least until you put them in a different building or change the circumstances slightly. Then their response time is the same as those without training.

Interestingly enough, students who have participated in periodic fire drills through different grade levels have typically learned different escape routes from the same building. These students have learned various ways to escape potential danger and tend to carry that "experience" with them to other environments.

The same principles of learning have been applied by professional athletes, public speakers, preachers, actors and the like. Practicing without the actual audience or other source of pressure being present allows you the time to focus in detail on your goal and program your creative mechanism through repetition to follow the habit and pathway you have established. The end result being that the new behavior becomes routine and normal.

Growth and fundamental levels of change tend to only occur when we are out of our comfort zone. A crisis is but a snapshot of a moment in time, all be it one we would prefer to avoid. But self-empowerment and creativity requires looking beyond that snapshot and envisioning what door of potential has just been opened.

Accepting the Challenge

The secret to overcoming any obstacle lies in confidently accepting the challenge and focusing your strengths. This means assuming an aggressive, goal oriented, positive attitude rather than a defensive, fearful, negative one.

The essence of this aggressive attitude is remaining goal oriented. Focus on your own positive goal with the intention of going through the crisis experience to achieve your goal. Do not get sidetracked by fear or the desire to run away and hide. If you do this, the crisis situation becomes the stimulus that releases the additional strength and power you need to accomplish your goal.

Why do some people break while others thrive in adversity? The answer is resilience, our ability to bounce back. Resilience is not something we are born with; it is a trait we develop through the experience of successfully navigating crises. The way you perceive an event determines how resilient you are. George Bonanno, the head of the Loss, Trauma, and Emotion Lab at Columbia University, says, "An event is not traumatic unless we experience it as such."

Psychiatrist Steven Wolin defines resiliency as "the capacity to rise above adversity." When something goes wrong, you must manage to stay in control rather than let the situation take over. Your thoughts shape your perceptions and behavior. Your perception of a negative event can turn it into a traumatic one or not. Your mindset, your thoughts, and how you frame reality, determine whether you will be traumatized by a crisis, or not.

Crises put our characters to the test. It's our choice that a better version of ourselves comes out of the storm. All crises are survivable. Putting things in perspective will help you focus on what you can control. As mentioned earlier, reframing is a powerful tool to help you cope with stressful events. It's more than just calling a crisis an opportunity. Instead of thinking, "Why is this happening to me?" think, "What can I learn from this event?" By reframing an incident, you recover control by shifting your role from victim to leader.

Words are powerful. The way we talk about the crisis has a direct impact on how we perceive what's going on. In the same way positive words create a positive response, negative words create an adverse effect. As neuroscientist Dr. Andrew Newberg explains, "The longer you concentrate on positive words, functions in the parietal lobe start to change, which changes your perception of yourself." Become more aware of the words you use. Reframe negative ones into positive words.

Using Your Emotional Intelligence

We live under the illusion that we have control over the events in our lives, but we don't. In 2020, that realization is more evident than ever. It's okay to feel afraid, anxious, or stressed out. Emotions are a natural response to external events, especially when we feel threatened. However, it is not okay is to let our emotions take over.

Neurologist J. A. Hadfield conducted an extensive study regarding how ordinary people seem to acquire extraordinary power in times of crisis. Hadfield noted that, when faced with a crisis situation, humans can tap into otherwise unseen power and strength to overcome obstacles, endure prolonged strain, and find a way out. What determines if we succeed or fail in the attempt is whether we accept the challenge presented by the crisis or cower in defeat.

We must manage how we respond. When we react to an external stimulus, there's a 90-second chemical process that happens in the body, putting us in full alert. After that time, the body flushes those chemicals away. This means that for 90 seconds, you can observe the process happening. You can experience, feel, and then "see" it how it goes away. You can react to this chemical alert, or you can wait until it's gone before you act.

The 90-second rule is a term coined by Dr. Jill Bolte Taylor in her book, *My Stroke of Insight*, to explain the nature and lifespan of an emotion. If you leave it uninterrupted by thoughts, you can quickly regain control of your response. Next time you are experiencing an emotional reaction, pause for a couple of minutes, consciously observe that moment, and don't let emotions dictate your response.

Is it a Crisis, or Just Another Obstacle?

As it turns out, there is historical precedent for recognizing, understanding, and then acting upon the obstacles that life throws at us. There is a way to turn them into opportunities. Iconic entrepreneurs like John D. Rockefeller, Thomas Edison and Steve Jobs all used this same formula when obstacles confronted them, even using, what for some were crisis situations, to fuel their immense ambitions. For them, the obstacle was the opportunity.

What follows are five strategies born of this tested and proven principle that we all can use to turn the challenges we face into great opportunities for ourselves and others. It's the one thing that all tremendously successful people have in common.

John D. Rockefeller was barely two years into his first job when the Panic of 1857 struck. Rockefeller could have become depressed and paralyzed by the unfortunate circumstances he faced. But instead of bemoaning the timing of the economic upheaval, he chose to perceive events differently than his peers. He looked at them as an opportunity to learn. He was inclined to look for opportunity in every disaster, as he once put it. Within 20 years of that first crisis, Rockefeller alone controlled 90 percent of the oil market.

Like Rockefeller, today's entrepreneurs live in turbulent times. Instead of letting our perception of events cloud our judgment, we can look to companies like LinkedIn and Microsoft, that were both founded during times of economic crisis. When others become lost worrying about a competitor's latest acquisition or an investor having a fit, we can channel Rockefeller's coolness under pressure and look for the opportunity in a crisis.

Steve Jobs was famous for what observers called his "reality distortion field," which made him dismissive of phrases like "It can't be done." When he ordered a special kind of glass for the first iPhone, manufacturers were dismayed at the aggressive deadline. "Don't be afraid," Jobs said. "You can do it. Get your mind around it. You can do it."

Nearly overnight, manufacturers transformed their facilities into glassmaking behemoths, and within six months they had made enough for the whole first run of the phone. His insistence pushed them past what they thought was possible.

We can choose to reject our first judgments and the objections that spring out of them by insisting that obstacles are in fact malleable not concrete. Like, Apple's leader we must have faith in our ability to make something where there was nothing before. To companies like Facebook and Google in their startup years, the idea that no one had ever done something was a good thing. It meant there was an opportunity to own it themselves.

When Thomas Edison's entire research and production campus burned to the ground, he didn't get angry or become despondent. Instead, he became energized and invigorated. He saw the complete destruction of the building as an opportunity to rebuild his lab into a more functional space. In only three weeks the factory was partially back up and running, all because Edison focused on the opportunity instead of the crisis.

In our own lives, we can follow Edison's example when we lose a job, or an employee unexpectedly leaves our company. When Jack Dorsey was replaced as CEO at Twitter, he didn't become paralyzed or depressed. Instead, he accepted it and went on to found Square, one of the largest payment-processing startups in the world. We don't benefit from tears, anger or despair. We always get something out of passionate intensity and exceptional focus and imagination.

You might not see yourself as exceptional; neither did most of these men and women. They were not academics, but people of action. But the essence of success is action, making good on the ability to turn the obstacles in life upside down with our minds.

Author and investor Tim Ferriss refers to resilience as his "operating system" and, in the tradition of those who came before him, he has successfully driven its adoption throughout Silicon Valley. We too can follow his example and use what others see as roadblocks as fuel for our ambitions and inevitable success.

Practical Application: Remember that the key to managing any crisis is how YOU DECIDE to react. Using your hindsight, write down one or two crises from your past when you were able to see an opportunity to make things better for yourself or someone else.

Chapter 11

Living Longer and Happier

"It's not the blowing of the wind that determines our destination, it's the set of the sail."

— Jim Rohn

In the process of living, the winds of life and circumstances blow on us all in an unending flow that touches each of our lives. What guides us to different destinations in life is determined by the way we choose to set our particular sail. The way that each of us thinks makes the major difference in where each of us arrive. The same winds of life blow on us all. The major difference is the set of the sail.

Sailing is almost a perfect metaphor for describing how life works. Did you know that a sailboat can sail against the wind? Using a technique called tacking, a skilled sailor can zigzag back and forth at a 45° angle, and still make forward progress, even against a headwind. Tacking requires skill, and it takes a while. But it can be done.

Sailboats need wind, that's true. But it's not the direction of the wind that determines where the vessel ends up, it's the set of the sail. And that's under the control of the captain. Each of us has our own ship to captain and a set amount of time on the water. Plenty is left up to us: our destination, our route, and how we set our sails. One big thing is not up to us, though, and that's the wind.

The wind represents the stuff we can't control: our past, the actions of others, and random events. Sometimes, the wind is directly at our back, and we barely need to unfurl our sails to be carried along. Everyone gets a tailwind like this from time to time, and some folks always seem to have one. Other times, we face a punishing headwind. Most of the time, the wind is somewhere in the middle, coolly indifferent.

The wind seems like it matters more than it really does. A skilled sailor can use any wind to his or her advantage, as we've learned. The problem is, it's really tempting to hope for a favorable wind instead of becoming a better sailor. We all fall prey to this all the time. We hit a rough patch in some aspect of our lives, and instead of focusing on personal growth and improving our situation. We get distracted by thoughts like "It's not fair," or "I hope things pick up soon," or "If I wait long enough, something's bound to change."

The only tool we have to harness the wind is the sail: our personal philosophy toward life. We can't do anything about the wind. But we have total control over our sails. A strong tailwind is a rare treat, but if you insist on waiting for it, you will make little progress. Don't just wait for opportunities to drop in your lap. Many people have done more with less than you have, and many people have done less with more than you have.

You can control what you focus on. And you'll get better results if you focus on what you can control. The wind is always changing, and all sails need frequent adjustment. You can't read a couple books on personal development and expect permanent change. There is no such thing as "set it and forget it," so check your course often.

What Are Your Goals?

In the same way that the same wind blow on us all, we all face similar circumstances in our lives. We all face difficulties and challenges. We all have those moments when, in spite of our best planning and efforts, things just seem to fall apart. In the final analysis, it is not what happens that determines the quality of our lives, it is what we choose to do when we have struggled to set the sail and then discover, after all of our efforts, the wind has changed direction.

When the winds change, we must change. We must struggle to our feet once more and reset our sail in a manner that will steer us toward the destination of our own choosing and desire. The set of the sail, how we think and how we choose to respond, has a far greater capacity to destroy our lives than any crisis or obstacle we face.

How quickly and responsibly you respond to adversity is far more important than the adversity itself. Once you discipline yourself to understand this, you will understand and will likely agree that the great challenge in life is to control your thinking.

Learning to reset your sail when the winds of life change, rather than allowing yourself to be blown in a direction you did not purposely choose, requires the development of discipline and goals.

When you consider the goals you have set for your life, career, family, etc., ask yourself the following questions:

- What qualities do I already have that could and would help to meet that goal?
- What do I already know that could help me meet this goal?
- How can I position myself to gain the skills and knowledge that would help me achieve this goal?
- What choices along the way would give me opportunities to experience satisfaction, happiness, and fulfillment in ways that matter to me?
- Even if I don't meet this goal, will I still feel good about myself throughout the efforts I make to do so?

These questions are not only based on your strengths. They also guide you to make choices and create opportunities that help you experience healthier levels of fulfillment. Meeting the goals may or may not happen without some course correction along the way. That part depends on your desire and what you tell your creative mechanism.

Whatever the end result, your self-perception is sure to undergo powerful, positive transformations on many levels. Through learning how to practice acceptance and compassion toward yourself, you can develop a self-image that will help you unlock your hidden potential. It will involve establishing a powerful personal philosophy that positively influences all that you do, think, and decide.

If you can succeed in this worthy endeavor, the result will be a change in the course of your income, lifestyle, relationships, how you feel about the things you value, and how you perceive life's challenges. If you can alter the way you perceive, judge, and decide on the main issues in life, then you absolutely can change your life.

In this last chapter, I want to share with you some of my own beliefs and personal philosophy, not as a professional, but as a man, a husband, and a father.

I believe the "human" part of our classification as human beings, including the brain, nervous system, and physical body, is a sort of electrochemically powered, biological, goal oriented machine. I do not believe that we ARE machines. I believe it is the "being" part of our classification as human beings, that is our spirit or soul, that animates, controls, and directs the biological vehicle we inhabit while on this earth toward.

For many decades psychologists, biologists, physiologists, and others have acknowledged that there is some sort of essence or energy that "runs" the human machine. And that the amount of influence, or level of control it has, may explain why some individuals are more resistant to disease than others, why some people age faster than others, etc.

It was also obvious to the scientific world that the source of this essence is something other than the energy we get from the food we eat. Caloric energy does not explain why some individuals can recover from surgery faster than others or withstand greater psychological stress than others. We generally refer to those individuals as having a "strong constitution." According to Dr. Janet Hadfield, writes that, "clinical psychologists and others who regularly deal with the actual diseases of men, have tended towards the view that the source of power is to be regarded as some impulse that works through us, and is not of our own making." Whether we are to view this impulse as cosmic energy, the ether, or what some consider the Divine immanence in nature, is for the individual to name and outside the scope of this book.

Since as early as 1936, this "life force" has been established as fact. Dr. Hans Selye called it adaptation energy. Throughout our lives we are called upon to adapt to stressful situations. Living is a process of continual adaptation to our environment. The term adaptation energy was coined to identify that which is consumed by the process of adapting in order to distinguish it from caloric energy we obtain from food that powers our physical body.

Creativity is certainly one of the characteristics of adaptive energy or life force. And the essence of creativity is moving forward toward a goal. Creative and driven personalities need more life force. As a group, creative people such as researchers, inventors, artists, writers and philosophers also tend to live longer and remain productive longer than non-creative workers.

This is why life coaches, counselors, and others encourage their clients to develop an enthusiasm for life. Create a need for more life and your adaptive energy will see that you have it. Faith, courage, interest, optimism, and looking forward to reaching a goal brings us new purpose and more life. Conversely, futility, pessimism, frustration, and living in the past are not only characteristic of old age, they contribute to it.

Many individuals, especially men, decline rapidly after retirement from the workforce. They often feel, with encouragement from seemingly everyone around them, like their active and productive life is complete and their job is done. Consequently, they often have little to look forward to, become bored and inactive.

Many retirees suffer a loss of self-esteem because they feel left out of things; not important anymore. They tend to develop a self-image of a useless, used up, has been. Consequently, many die within a year or so after retirement. It is not retiring from a job that kills these people, it's retiring from life.

It is the feelings of uselessness and the subsequent dampening of self-esteem, courage, and self-confidence which our present societal attitude helps encourage. Most of these perceptions are based on outmoded ideas from the likes of Sigmund Freud and others that were summarized in the disproven cliché that "you can't teach an old dog new tricks." Tell that to those enjoying successful second and third careers in their 50s, 60s, and 70s.

Final Thoughts

In sharing my personal beliefs, I must also say that, at some level, I believe in miracles. I have written extensively about *what* can happen, and *how* my life is different as a result of practicing these time tested and proven concepts. But I will not pretend to know or even understand *why* they work, or how the Life Force uses the servomechanism to steer us toward our goals.

I do not understand how, what I consider Divine Design, causes cuts to heal with natural tissue that grows back thicker and stronger than the original. While I know *that* the subconscious mind influences our conscious mind, I would not pretend to know *how* it works. For me, the subconscious mind and the Spirit are the same.

Religious teaching around the world share a story of a prophet lost in the desert who was hungry, so God lowered a sheet from heaven full of food. But the prophet refused the food because the religious leaders of the time had taught it was "unclean." Whereas God admonished him not call "unclean" anything God had provided him. Yet today, some doctors, scientists, and self-aggrandized people turn up their noses at anything that smacks of religion or faith. Similarly, many clergy and otherwise spiritualists have the same attitude about science and medicine.

Regardless of personal religious or scientific belief, most would agree the goal is more years of life and more life in our years. I believe that there is One Life, one source, but that this One Life has many avenues of expression and can manifest itself in many forms. If our objective is to get more living out of life, maybe we should not limit the ways in which Life may choose to come to us or proclaim ourselves unworthy of Life's attention.

The ideas and exercises in this book have helped thousands of practitioners for more than a century, including the author, develop a better self-image, overcome family heritage and socioeconomics, and be a better person all around. It is my sincere hope it will do the same for you.

What will you paint on the canvas of your life, before you run out of space, or your paint dries up?

About the Author

Bill Riggs is a best-selling author with expertise in a variety of topics including the impact of societal ideologies like socialism and woke culture and leadership principles including the Pygmalion Effect. Riggs' work often delves into the intersections of personal, social, and professional development, framed through practical advice and personal experience. His writing tends to address both modern challenges and historical perspectives, offering insight into leadership, societal shifts, and personal responsibility.

Bibliography

Bandura A. Social foundations of thought and action: A social cognitive theory. Englewood Cliffs, NJ: Prentice-Hall: 1986.

Bargh JA, editor. Social psychology and the unconscious: The automaticity of higher mental processes. Psychology Press; Philadelphia: 2006.

Bargh JA, Gollwitzer PM, Lee-Chai A, Barndollar K, Troetschel R. The automated will: Unconscious activation and pursuit of behavioral goals. Journal of Personality and Social Psychology. 2001;81:1004–1027.

Baumeister, R. F., & Vohs, K. D. (2007). Self-regulation, ego depletion, and motivation. *Social and Personality Psychology Compass, 1*, 115-128.

Boutelle KN, Bouton ME. Implications of learning theory for developing programs to decrease overeating. Appetite. 2015;93:62-74. doi:10.1016/j.appet.2015.05.013

Dawkins R. The selfish gene. Oxford University Press; New York: 1976.

Dennett DC. Consciousness explained. Little, Brown; Boston: 1991.

Dennett DC. Darwin's dangerous idea: Evolution and the meanings of life. Simon & Schuster; New York: 1995.

Dijksterhuis A, Chartrand TL, Aarts H. Automatic behavior. In: Bargh JA, editor. Social psychology and the unconscious: The automaticity of higher mental processes. Psychology Press; Philadelphia: 2007.

Dunsmoor JE, Murphy GL. Categories, concepts, and conditioning: how humans generalize fear. Trends Cogn Sci (Regul Ed). 2015;19(2):73-7. doi:10.1016/j.tics.2014.12.003

Fitzsimons GM, Bargh JA, Baumeister RF, Vohs KD. Handbook of self-regulation: Research, theory, and applications. Guilford Press; New York: 2004. Automatic self-regulation; pp. 151–170.

Gazzaniga M. The social brain. Basic Books; New York: 1985.

James W. Principles of psychology. Vol. 2. Holt; New York: 1890.

Libet B. Unconscious cerebral initiative and the role of conscious will in voluntary action. Behavioral and Brain Sciences. 1986;8:529–566.

Locke EA, Latham GP. Building a practically useful theory of goal setting and task performance: A 35 year odyssey. American Psychologist. 2002;57:705–717.

Martin, B. (2018). Challenging Negative Self-Talk. *Psych Central.* Retrieved on August 18, 2020, from https://psychcentral.com/lib/challenging-negative-self-talk.

Rohn, J. (2011). My Philosophy for Successful Living. No Dream Too Big Publishing, LLC; Melrose, FL.

Silverman K, Jarvis BP, Jessel J, Lopez AA. Incentives and Motivation. Transl Issues Psychol Sci. 2016;2(2):97-100. doi:10.1037/tps0000073

Wegner DM. The Illusion of Conscious Will. MIT Press; Cambridge, MA: 2002.

www.ingramcontent.com/pod-product-compliance
Lightning Source LLC
LaVergne TN
LVHW091118150826
845673LV00002B/880

* 9 7 9 8 2 3 0 2 6 8 9 4 9 *